"This book offers an authentic and powerful Palestinian perspective on the killing fields of Gaza through an impressive fusion of historical analysis intertwined with moving personal anecdotes. In *Banging on the Walls of the Tank*, the people of Gaza appear as they really are: resilient and incredibly courageous in the face of a genocidal campaign against them. It is clear from this moving collection that one cannot wipe out Gaza as one would not be able to expunge Palestine as a whole as an idea, a nation, and a country. This is a must-read for anyone who wants to comprehend fully what it means to live in the biggest prison on earth, constantly in danger of annihilation."

ILAN PAPPE, author of *The Ethnic Cleansing of Palestine*

"This book brings us back to ourselves, humbled, enraged, and reminded of why Gaza is all of Palestine at once, and the centre of the world. For those of us who have watched in bewilderment the silence of the world through year after year of starvation by siege in Gaza, and war after war, Haidar Eid brings all the memories back with *Banging on the Walls of the Tank*. For those just tuning in, it is all that you need to understand what brought us here and to move us to the liberated future we yearn for. Listen to this insurgent voice of Gaza, to its fiery depth and pained defiance. Gaza can teach us all that is worth knowing. How to be free. How to be human."

DR. JAMILA J. GHADDAR, assistant professor, Department of Media Studies, University of Amsterdam

"Haidar Eid's essays from inside the Israeli siege and wars on Gaza in the twenty-first century are a journey alongside Palestine's enduring writers for freedom. The book's title is taken from Ghassan Kanafani's iconic story of the three Palestinian refugees who suffocated unheard in a truck, Mahmoud Darwish's love poem, *Silence for Gaza* opens the book, and Eid's life's writing is steeped in Edward Said's work. This is a book to discover Gaza today."

VICTORIA BRITTAIN, journalist and author

BANGING ON THE WALLS OF THE TANK

BANGING ON THE WALLS OF THE TANK

DISPATCHES FROM GAZA

HAIDAR EID

Between the Lines
Toronto

First published in 2025 by
Between the Lines
401 Richmond Street West, Studio 281
Toronto, Ontario · M5V 3A8 · Canada
1-800-718-7201 · www.btlbooks.com

Library and Archives Canada Cataloguing in Publication
Title: Banging on the walls of the tank : dispatches from Gaza / Haidar Eid.
Names: Eid, Haidar, author
Description: Includes index.
Identifiers: Canadiana (print) 20250108038 | Canadiana (ebook) 20250108046 | ISBN 9781771136754 (softcover) | ISBN 9781771136761 (EPUB)
Subjects: LCSH: Gaza Strip—History—21st century.
Classification: LCC DS110.G3 E33 2025 | DDC 956.94/3—dc23

Cover and text design by DEEVE

Printed in Canada

We acknowledge for their financial support of our publishing activities: the Government of Canada; the Canada Council for the Arts; and the Government of Ontario through the Ontario Arts Council, the Ontario Book Publishers Tax

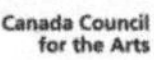

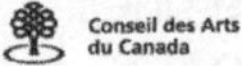

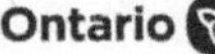

To the memory of Hind Rajab and all the thousands of anonymous children who died in the Gaza extermination camp and those who remain under the rubble.

Gaza is not the most beautiful city.
Its shore is not bluer than the shores of Arab cities.
Its oranges are not the most beautiful in the
Mediterranean basin.

Gaza is not the richest city.
It is not the most elegant or the biggest, but it equals the history of an entire homeland because it is more ugly, impoverished, miserable, and vicious in the eyes of enemies. Because it is the most capable, among us, of disturbing the enemy's mood and his comfort. Because it is his nightmare. Because it is mined oranges, children without a childhood, old men without old age and women without desires.

Because of all this it is the most beautiful, the purest and richest among us and the one most worthy of love.

—Mahmoud Darwish, "Silence for Gaza"

CONTENTS

xiii Foreword by Richard Falk
xxv Prologue

Gaza 2009

TWENTY-TWO DAYS

3 January 22, 2009—Sharpeville 1960, Gaza 2009
8 February 11, 2009—Culture of Resistance vs. Defeat
14 November 19, 2009—From Gaza to Obama: An Open Letter
18 July 27, 2010—The Enduring Siege

Gaza 2012

HISTORY REPEATS ITSELF

25 November 20, 2012—Gaza 2012!
28 May 28, 2013—Personal Reflections on the Nakba

Gaza 2014

THE WORLD'S BIGGEST GRAVEYARD

33 February 18, 2014—The Alternative Is BDS!
36 July 12, 2014—Signposts on the Road to Liberation
41 July 31, 2014—The Rape of Gaza
45 August 27, 2014—The Othering of Gaza
49 February 12, 2015—On Gaza and Global Rage
53 April 2, 2015—Israel: Mainstream Western Media's Blind Spot
58 April 6, 2016—Palestinian Reflections on Israel's Hysterical Attack on BDS
61 June 16, 2017—One Question Left in Gaza: Death by Massacre or Lack of Electricity?
65 July 14, 2017—Gaza and the Failure of the National Project

69 October 20, 2017—Pessoptimistic Reflections from Besieged Gaza

Gaza 2018

LAND DAY MASSACRE

73 2018—Gaza in a World Without Walls
79 April 5, 2018—What Next for Gaza After Israel's Land Day Massacre?
82 April 12, 2018—Standing Up to Apartheid: Contextualizing the Great March of Return
85 May 14, 2018—On the Seventieth Anniversary of the Nakba: Reflections of a Palestinian Refugee
89 May 16, 2018—Why I Marched on May 14 in Gaza near the Israeli Fence
93 June 14, 2018—It Is Time to Levy Sanctions Against Israel
96 July 22, 2018—Israel Has Finally Come Out as an Ethno-Religious State
100 July 24, 2018—Back to the Future: The Great March of Return
104 August 3, 2018—Israel's Policies in Gaza Are Genocidal
108 October 12, 2018—Fragmented Thoughts from the Eastern Fence of the Gaza Open-Air Prison
110 November 9, 2018—What Gaza Wants
112 May 6, 2019—Gaza Has Made Its Choice: It Will Continue to Resist
116 November 20, 2019—The Only Remaining Hope in Gaza Is Knowing This Nightmare Can Be Brought to an End
119 June 20, 2020—What Needs to Be Done

Gaza 2021

WEDHA STREET MASSACRE

125 May 16, 2021—Israel's Wehda Street Massacre Shows It Seeks to Annihilate Us. We Won't Let It
128 May 27, 2021—An Apartheid Déjà Vu

132 December 10, 2021—The Construction of Israel's Gaza Concentration Camp Is Complete
135 November 21, 2022—Reflections from Gaza After Israel's Elections

Gaza 2023

GENOCIDE

139 October 10, 2023—Our Warsaw Uprising Moment
143 October 15, 2023—From Gaza We Ask You to Stand Up Against Genocide!
147 October 30, 2023—"Demise of Official Arab Solidarity with Palestine"
150 November 27, 2023—A Ceasefire in a Time of Genocide
154 December 3, 2023—Leaving Gaza
157 December 9, 2023—Why Does America Hate Us?
161 December 30, 2023—On the Gaza "Shoah" and the "Banality of Evil"
164 January 12, 2024—From a Palestinian in Gaza, Thank You South Africa!
168 January 26, 2024—ICJ Israel Decision: A New World Order in the Making
172 May 1, 2024—The Genocide in Gaza Will Also Be the End of Israel
175 June 9, 2024—My Nuseirat
178 June 28, 2024—War on Gaza: The World Has Abandoned Us. What Can We Do?
181 July 13, 2024—Now the Anemone Flowers Will Decorate His Grave
184 The One Year Anniversary of October 7: Personal Reflections

189 Epilogue

193 Acknowledgements
195 Notes
199 Index

Foreword

THE POLITICAL IS INEVITABLY PERSONAL

I have read many discerning and moving books on Palestine over the last fifty years, but none has spoken to me as forcefully and persuasively as this short volume of opinion pieces written by Haidar Eid from 2009 to the present. The prophetic insight of these dispatches and their cumulative impact offer readers a vivid Palestinian narrative of tragic suffering and the heroic resistance of the Gazan population to Israel's occupation, settler colonialism, apartheid, and genocide, as well as a pervasive Israeli reliance on collective punishment of Palestinians.

Banging on the Walls of the Tank, a reliable interpretation not filtered and distorted by Western mainstream media, should be read by all those in the West who seek to understand the bitter realities of the Israel/Palestine struggle. Almost every page is enlivened by the author's uncannily memorable formulations of the true and awful nature of the Palestinian plight, which was desperate long before the horrifying real-time genocide that has unfolded in the form of daily atrocity spectacles ever since October 7. In his readable style and with the skill of a trustworthy storyteller, Eid offers insights rooted in his direct experiences as a Gaza refugee, expositor of Palestinian steadfastness, resistance activist, witness, and survivor.

Contextualizing October 7

These dispatches, written since 2009 in response to the evolving bloody tactics and criminality of the Israeli occupation, are both an anticipation of the October 7 attack and a condemnation of the Israeli genocidal response. An aspect of the originality and significance of Eid's presentation is it convincingly demonstrates that Israel has harboured an apartheid ideology and practice from the time of its birth. This is long before the most influential human rights organizations (including Human Rights Watch and Amnesty International) dared issue reports, as they did in 2021, that fully documented the allegations that Israel was systematically applying apartheid policies and practices to administer the occupation. Israel also relied upon discriminatory internal regulatory laws to subjugate all Palestinians who were directly subject to Israeli sovereignty, including those living in post-1948 Israel as citizens. These domestic laws were supplemented by exclusionary nationality laws and practices relied upon by Israel to deny Palestinian refugees a right of return, as bestowed by international law and confirmed by the United Nations General Assembly (UNGA) Resolution 194 (December 11, 1948), while at the same time granting birthright Jews an unlimited right of return regardless of any link to Israel.

Eid's dissent from pro-Israeli orthodoxy in Europe and North America extends to his important assessment that Israel's supposed "disengagement" from Gaza in 2005 was deceptively presented to the world as a move toward peace. What was not told was that this Israeli unilateral initiative was coupled with Israeli administered border control that effectively imprisoned 2.3 million Gazans in their own homeland. Such confinement was later cruelly reinforced by a punitive siege that converted Gaza into what became known as the world's largest ever concentration camp. The impact over time of these oppressive conditions are characterized by Eid, borrowing from historian Ilan Pappé,[1] as "incremental genocide." This importantly demarcates the "before" and "after" of October 7 as one of continuity rather than as totally discontinuous, coming out of the blue, as Israel, followed by the West, desperately wants us to believe up to this day. It is obvious that Israel devoted much attention to decontextualizing October 7 to avoid the implications of the pre-October 7 realities of apartheid and incremental genocide, so persuasively delineated by Eid, being taken into account when evaluating the Hamas attack.

Eid is writing as a victim/survivor/activist as well as a journalist/intellectual of the before and after of the Gaza ordeal. For him, the sixteen months of direct, undisguised genocide that has preoccupied the world to an unprecedented degree was nothing fundamentally new but rather an intensification of what Gazans had been experiencing ever since 1967 in more attenuated forms. There is no doubt that incremental genocide would be virtually impossible to establish in a court of law as a distinct crime because of the difficulty of proving genocidal intent as compared to criminalizing what followed after October 7 as a violation of the Genocide Convention. The numerous undisguised assertions by Israel's top leaders easily met the rigorous legal standards of genocidal intent insisted upon by objective jurists. These words of genocidal incitement were combined with the crude, often sadistic, Israeli Defense Forces combat tactics relied upon to bring its helpless Palestinian adversary agonizingly close to the brink of extinction.

The Israeli discourse on October 7 also points its finger at Hamas, seeking its complete delegitimation by treating its attack as pure "terrorism," justifying extermination and relieving Israel of any pressure to obey the laws of war in its response. Eid challenges this Israeli rationalization by regarding the attack as both a justifiable and a legitimate form of resistance, especially in view of the context, which includes the Netanyahu performance at the UNGA a few weeks earlier during which he displayed a map with no Palestinian entity, an erasure of Palestine alongside the presumed establishment of Greater Israel. By taking these factors into account, Eid produces a revisionist view of October 7 that is more realistic and reflective of the values at stake.

There is a deeper significance to the way Eid establishes the context accounting for October 7. His approach is a necessary antidote to the Western hegemonic discourse, which denounced any assertion that the Palestinian attack was justifiable resistance to the provocative criminality of apartheid, several terrifying militarily inflicted massacres, and sixteen years of a cruelly punitive blockade whose constraints on imports could not be plausibly justified as a security measure while guaranteeing the misery of Palestinian lives in Gaza. Eid's book should be read as a corrective to the disgraceful performance of a mainstream media in the West that excluded all considerations of context from its evaluation of the events of October 7 and declared justificatory acceptance of Israel's claimed entitlement to act in self-defence, echoing its coverup of overt recourse to genocide as nothing other than a necessary "security operation." This is a deliberate attempt to banish the word "genocide" from use in Western public discourse and mainstream media when reporting on Israel's totally dominant military capabilities in executing its indiscriminate rampage against the completely helpless civilian population of Gaza. Despite this effort to restore the discipline of pro-Israeli discourse, describing the Israeli violence as "genocide" has been gradually normalized in many societal and media venues, but not yet all.

Failures of Implementation: International Law and Universal Moral Standards

This linkage between what daily occurs on the ground in Gaza and the broader issues of toxic dysfunction that have long poisoned the Palestinian experience exposes the wilful impotence of what Eid generously terms the "international community," as if there was one. It is intolerable for Eid that outsiders, whether governments, international institutions, media, or even individuals, remain spectators, or worse, render aid and comfort to the perpetrators and their accomplices in carrying out this "crime of crimes." Along the way, Eid acknowledges that the Nazi Holocaust against Jews was similarly internationally tolerated, especially by the Western liberal democracies that have, since 1945, alleviated their guilt at the expense of the Palestinians, who pay for moral shortcomings for which they had no responsibility. Two massive wrongs never make things right; rather, as the poet Auden teaches, "those to whom evil is done / do evil in return."[2]

Israel's official occupation policy stressed putting the people of Gaza "on a diet," with just enough food to avoid death by starvation but not enough to enable nutritional health. Eid emphasizes the long denial of the right of return enjoyed by refugees after 1948 as affirmed in the UNGA Resolution 194. Any process of satisfying the requirements of international law would also necessitate the dismantling of the apartheid regime of control and ethno-religious claims of a Jewish supremist state.

Eid's Vision and Its Enemies

As Eid articulates his vision of a benevolent future for the Palestinian people, he sets forth its simple but far-reaching governance implications: a single secular state for both peoples from the river to the sea with equal rights for all resident ethnicities. For Eid, this is the one and only solution, an indirect repudiation of the two-state delusion as well as his complete rejection of an Israeli one-state apartheid Greater Israel.

Eid does far more than relate the horrors of incremental genocide. He not only condemns the Israeli perpetrators but severely incriminates their complicit supporters, who supplied the weaponry and funding that sustains the mighty military capabilities of Israel and gave diplomatic credence to it is flagrant defiance of international law. This is more than critique, it is also a rejection of the only pathway Eid envisions as leading to peace with justice for the Palestinians, and even Jews. Such a solution, which will strike many jaded souls as "utopian" or both unattainable and unacceptable, rests on the simple major premise of fulfilling Palestinian rights under international law. In the Palestinian case, this means, among other policy alterations, lifting the draconian blockade of Gaza that has made the daily existence of its inhabitants (two-thirds of whom are refugees) a life of misery, one deliberately "engineered" by Israeli tacticians who "mow the lawn," a term officials in Tel Aviv use to refer to Israel's massive military attacks, which are properly undertaken whenever the vitality of Gazan's resistance activism seems to pose security threats, regardless of whether it is armed struggle or nonviolent civil action.

Eid's dispatches are written with the passion and experience of someone who has lived as a refugee since 1964, when he was born in Gaza. His parents lived in the Nuseirat Refugee Camp after they were forced, in 1948, to leave their home in the Palestinian village of Zarnouga. As the decades passed, they never gave up their expectation of one day returning to Zarnouga, even knowing it had been demolished. As they faced death, Eid's parents last wish was that at least their bodies could be returned to their village for burial; a wish that was denied; a wish that, even if granted, would be far from fulfilling the kind of return envisioned by international law.

That he grew up in a refugee household helps explain Eid's preoccupation with the exercise of the right of return of the five or six million Palestinians living as refugees as a necessary feature of any sustainable and acceptable peace process. And as such, it undoubtedly informs why he shows such contempt for the Oslo diplomacy initiated in 1993, a diplomacy that totally ignored, and implicitly rejected, this basic right embodied in international law. On other grounds, as well, Oslo justifiably reinforced his rejection of a Palestinian leadership that failed to insist on affirming the Palestinian entitlement to the most fundamental of human rights in the post-colonial era, the inalienable right of self-determination possessed by all peoples and claimed on behalf of every nation on the planet. Eid adopts a cynical view of the Palestinian Liberation Organization, which, by accepting the Oslo framework, sacrificed the future of Palestine for a seat at the far end of the negotiating table and the dubious "reward" of a photo op on the White House lawn; the photo used by the West to show the world the much celebrated but deeply misleading Arafat/Rabin handshake as a historic reconciliation that was never to be implemented. What followed the publicized initiation of Oslo diplomacy was, at best, a charade that dragged on long enough for Israel to expand its settler population to a politically irreversible level. Throughout, Israel has benefited from a "peace process" that was never about peace and which, while running its course, seriously harmed the Palestinians. The supervision of the negotiations by the overtly partisan US government should never have been accepted by the designated representatives of the Palestinian people, who defied reason by not insisting on neutral auspices. As Rashid Khalidi, among others, have shown, the United States never even pretended to be an honest broker of the Oslo Process, making no secret of situating itself in Israel's corner.[3]

Eid's perspective is formed by a blend of his multiple identities as victim, witness, survivor, activist, humanist, writer and journalist, university teacher, and public intellectual. This rare combination of experience and commitment contributes to making Eid an exemplary interpreter of the ongoing Palestinian ordeal. He is decidedly not a neutral observer; he is an undisguised and fully engaged "honest partisan" who develops a compelling Palestinian account of why the Palestinian ordeal came about and was allowed to happen. While his observations are avowedly one-sided, this lack of balance, oddly, provides a more objective approach because it is congruent with the realities of Gaza if tested by the evidence, regulative norms of law and morality, and proclaimed values at stake. As such, it presents readers with a happy contrast to the brainwashing pretensions of such influential media platforms as the *New York Times* or *The Economist*, which claim balance but, when it comes to reporting on Israel/Palestine, are more accurately perceived as sophisticated instruments of state propaganda.

Even without the benefit of being confronted by the pre-October 7 historical, legal, and ethical context, public protest began to mount, including in the centres of Israeli support in North America and Western Europe, as Israel continued the genocide unabated, refusing to heed growing public calls for ceasefires and constraint. Pro-Palestinian protests erupted on many university campuses but were quickly countered by Israeli donor leverage and governmental pressures, especially in the US. With the advent of Trump in 2025, pro-Palestinian activism on campuses and elsewhere faced renewed challenges, and not only in the US but also throughout Europe, reflecting a political swing to the ultraright.

Valuing and Learning from the Eid Perspective

What also makes Eid's commentary exceptional is the authenticity of his voice, shaped by his intense experiences since his birth in 1964. His work is further informed by channelling the wisdom of profound and enraged Palestinian cultural icons, referencing the insights of Ghassan Kanafani, Mahmoud Darwish, and Edward Said, as well as making good use of anti-colonial writings drawn from authors in the Global South. It should be instructive for all readers that Eid derives his inspirational *political* guidance from these *cultural* sources rather than from the Palestinian political leaders that he holds co-responsible for misleading their own people in various self-destructive ways. Eid is appalled by the willingness of the Palestinian leaders anointed by the West to accept what he calls "bread crumbs" rather than insisting on liberation and basic rights as conferred by international law; law that is never acknowledged by Israel or enforced by either the UN or responsible geopolitical statecraft, ineptly overseen by the United States since the end of the Cold War, that tended to favour geopolitical and strategic interests to legal, moral, and even prudent restraint. The most tainted bread crumb, in Eid's reflections, is the idea of the acceptance of a permanently demilitarized Palestinian statehood on 22 percent of historic Palestine, especially considering that, in 1947, Palestinians rejected the dubious UN partition resolution that split the country—but at least awarded Palestinian with 45 percent of the land.

Eid is deeply influenced by the successful, analogous struggle against the hegemonic racism and settler colonialism of apartheid South Africa. He believes that the lessons of this earlier struggle can be adapted and applied to Palestinian circumstances, embracing the famous dictum, often attributed to Italian philosopher Antonio Gramsci, "pessimism of the intellect, optimism of the will," which distinguishes the rational understanding of political injustices from an emotional reassurance that a just outcome will emerge from the struggle of the Palestinian people. In addressing this tension from my outlook, my rational self is less confident than Eid about the sufficiency of the South African model of liberation. I believe that Palestinian liberation will remain impossible unless it overcomes the primacy of adverse geopolitics (shaped by strategic interests rather than by a willingness to respect the rule of law and universally affirmed moral norms). These currently unregulated forces empower the Islamophobic complicity of the white West and are currently aligned with the Zionist networks in the West that have exerted an unhealthy influence over policy formation at national, regional, and global levels.

Giving equal attention to matters of political will, I am also encouraged by anti-colonial success stories. This reading of the recent historical record echoes Eid's interpretations and, before him, Said's. Both thinkers deeply theorized a belief that the side that controls "the high moral ground" in the end prevails politically over the side that dominates the battlefield due to its military superiority. In my terminology, and in keeping with Eid's assessments, Palestine is winning this Legitimacy War and is on its way to an emancipatory future, although with much suffering and devastation on the road to such a political outcome. This guardedly hopeful outlook assumes Palestinian perseverance for as long as it takes, which Israel is ceaselessly working to undermine and weaken by its recourse to the most extreme methods of violence in the combat zones and to dirty tricks overseas, including "weaponizing antisemitism" as a policy tool of combat.

In Conclusion

The title of Eid's book, borrowed from a poignant line in Kanafani's novel *Men in the Sun*, would strike most international readers as enigmatic and obscure. Eid informs us that these words have become a popular slogan of Palestinian resistance fighters, conveying the vital message, "If you want to live, make noise"; that is, resist, but if ready to die in body or spirit, stay quiet. Such is Eid's fighting spirit. His noise is a challenge to all everywhere to act on behalf of the Palestinian struggle within our respective spaces before it is too late. And as a fitting indictment, Eid's last words in the epilogue again echo those of Kanafani: "Gazans have been banging on the walls of the Gaza concentration camp since 1948," and still nothing happens by way of rescue, much less liberation. Silence almost everywhere, especially shameful among Arab regimes neighbouring besieged Gaza, is reinforced by the timidities of the Arab League.

For Eid, Arab silence is not broken by uttering words of condemnation unless accompanied by coercive actions. In this sense, Eid's own journey has led him and his family to take refuge in South Africa in recent months, the country that has acted more substantively than any other against Israel since October 7 by submitting a graphic complaint to the International Court of Justice (ICJ) alleging Israeli violations of the Genocide Convention. Unsurprisingly, Eid in exile insists that Palestinian liberation must take the form of a single secular constitutional and democratic state with recognized borders encompassing the whole of mandate Palestine. This affirmation is coupled with a total rejection of the dangerous fiction of co-existence and accommodation that is based on the mutual acceptance of a neutered Palestinian mini state that would be permanently demilitarized and otherwise left at the mercy of a highly militarized and racist Israel.

Secondly for Eid, a present grounding of realistic hope in this particular liberation struggle must be predominantly based on the activation of *people* rather than the good will and energies of *governments* and their institutions. This leads Eid to stress, with a sense of urgency, the role of solidarity initiatives throughout the world as typified by the Boycott, Divestment, Sanctions (BDS) campaign. He strongly endorses BDS as a principal modality of

Palestinian prospects ever since its initiation in 2005, when it began as a collective action with the backing of 170 Palestinian civil society organizations. In effect, liberation from settler colonialism in the historical present can move toward victory only when people in strategic countries around the world are sufficiently mobilized to exert transformative pressures on governments and the international community to undo the political and economic ties that bind them to the oppressor.

Eid is lucidly persuasive in his refusal to accept the common refrain that there are "two sides" in recent debates about Israeli tactics and goals. Zionist liberals especially would have us so believe, evading the central reality that this is a classic struggle, with its distinctive features of the oppressed against the oppressor and its complicit allies. Eid is seeking a crucial rectification of the asymmetrical nature of the struggle, which continues to be highly controversial in the West but seems vital to act upon if non-Palestinians are to support a genuinely just and sustainable peace. This view expresses a radical challenge to the status quo as its realization requires the rejection of the Zionist Project of Jewish supremist prerogatives in a distinct state as the essential precondition that could enable the two peoples to live together as equals. Eid's vision of liberation does not include the forced departure (in effect, an ethnic cleansing) of Jews or the destruction of Israel as a state, but it does require major adjustments: a fundamental reconstruction of its internal race relations, an abandonment of Zionist ideology, ethnic equality of treatment in nationality and citizenship laws, and quite likely the naming of the emergent one-state entity to signify the rejection of an ethnic statehood for either people.

Gruesome patterns of Israeli abuses over the years are further confirmed by Eid's own existential encounters with Israel's prolonged dehumanizing and sadistic treatment of the people of Gaza, especially its children. His prose is written not with ink but with the blood of the innocents, undoubtedly a tearful recounting of very concrete incidents involving family members, close friends, neighbours. Eid is unflinching in his determination to bring Israel's brutalizing behaviour out into the open by bearing anguished witness to targeted killings of innocent children by

Israeli snipers and to high tech weapons of war that killed whole families trapped in their homes and devastated entire residential neighbourhoods during Israel's massive incursions, characterized as "massacres," in 2008–09, 2012, 2014, 2018, and frequently, on a smaller scale, in the lead-up to the full-scale genocidal response to October 7. In a significant conceptual move, Eid follows Pappé in presenting these years preceding that pivotal day as incremental genocide. This reality posed for every Palestinian an ultimate choice between the dangers of resistance and the humiliations of submission to the harsh apartheid constraints of Israeli control.

What makes this book truly groundbreaking, aside from its chronicling of witnessing in ways that impressively counteract the propagandistic decontextualization of October 7, is its clarity when it comes to a critique of the mainstream diagnosis of the Palestinian struggle and accompanying positive prescriptions about the path to a Palestinian victory emerging from the piles of rubble signifying Gaza after enduring these months of genocide.

Even though the provisional rulings of the ICJ on January 26, 2024, did nothing to change the facts on the ground, it should be read as an authoritative affirmation of the legitimacy of the Palestinian struggle and a heartfelt juridical lament for the accompanying humanitarian catastrophe still befalling Gaza. It undoubtedly helped motivate Eid to express the optimism of his will by the dramatic assertion in the epilogue that "Israel is now on the verge of collapse."

RICHARD FALK
Santa Barbara, California
30 January 2025

PROLOGUE

> Zionists executed the psychological coup of the century by taking Palestine from the Arabs and then pretending Jews were Arab victims.
>
> —Roberta Strauss Feuerlicht, *The Fate of the Jews*

This book is both personal and political, my testimony of being a Palestinian refugee residing in what has been called the largest open-air prison on earth but also a voice from within offering a way out of the manufactured quagmire in Palestine. My decision to put together in a single book the articles and essays I wrote and published during the Israeli onslaughts on Gaza and the hermetic blockade that has been imposed on it since 2007 was inspired by the 2021 image of Amara Abu Ouf, who raised a V for victory sign while being rescued from under the rubble of a building levelled to the ground by an American-made Israeli F-16 in what became known as the Wehda Street massacre. Different from mainstream ahistorical coverage of the unfolding events in Gaza, I try to contextualize and historicize them. This is why the articles I have gathered here are ordered chronologically and vary in their take on the events.

I am an academic teaching literature and cultural studies at a Gaza-based Palestinian university, but I am also a Boycott, Divestment, and Sanctions (BDS) activist calling for the isolation of the only remaining apartheid regime on earth. I have been affected by the works of the likes of Steve Biko, Frantz Fanon, Aimé Césaire, Amilcar Cabral, and most certainly Ghassan Kanafani and Edward Said, among other towering intellectuals and activists of our (post)colonial world. But I must add the impact of my stay and studies in post-apartheid South Africa as one of the most inspiring experiences of my life as an oppressed Palestinian and an activist. With the publication of Amnesty International, Human Rights Watch, Btselem's reports, and the United Nations Economic and Social Commission for Western Asia (ESCWA) findings before them, not to mention the passing of the notorious ultra-racist nation-state law by the Israeli Knesset, Israel has been confirmed as an apartheid state. And settler-colonial apartheid states thrive and survive on the dehumanization of the "barbarian" native. Hence, Gaza.

The point of this book is not to offer the last word on what has been termed by right-wing politicians and some mainstream media outlets as "the Gaza conflict" but rather to map a way out of the catastrophe created by Israel and provide a trajectory of personal and political involvement in the Palestinian struggle for freedom.

How many books have been written by Gazans about Gaza in English? Where is the voice of Gazans? Why does mainstream media hide the fact that the overwhelming majority of Gazans are refugees ethnically cleansed from their Palestinian villages and towns in 1948 by Israel? We are portrayed as either villains or victims, but never human beings with full rights to freedom. We are aware of the fact that we are the centre of so much attention, yet, ironically, we are never heard from; we are not given the permission to narrate our own narrative, as Edward Said put it.[4]

Why This Book?

The late Palestinian writer, Ghassan Kanafani was one of the first anti-colonial intellectuals in Palestine to emphasize the need for writing our own narrative—albeit of resistance and *sumud*.* In his heartbreaking novel *Men in the Sun*,[5] written ten years after the Nakba, the story of three voiceless Palestinian refugees in exile who move from Jordan to Iraq to be smuggled into Kuwait, where they wish to earn money and bring an end to their poverty. The men are smuggled in a tanker truck, with the driver promising, "You'll get into the tank five minutes from the frontier, and fifty meters beyond it, you'll climb out." But when the truck is unexpectedly pulled over at one of the borders, the men are left inside for much longer than anticipated. The driver gets on the road again, worried about the people in the back but unable to check on them. When he reaches the next stop, he opens the back to find the three men

* steadfastness

dead. Anguished, he cries, "Why didn't you bang on the walls of the tank? Why didn't you say anything? Why?"

"Banging on the walls of the tank" has become one of the most loved metaphors in Palestinian discourse of resistance. It is a reference to making noise in order to be heard, to draw the attention of the world to one's suffering caused by imperialist powers, in general, and Israeli colonization of Palestine, in particular.

This is why I have decided to publish this book in English; in the hope of continuing a legacy started by the likes of Ghassan Kanafani, Edward Said, Fadwa Touqan, and Mahmoud Darwish—to mention but a very few Palestinian intellectuals and writers who, to our mind, represent the deliberately unheard Palestinian voice. But, within the context of Gaza, we need voices that have lived "The Horror! The Horror!"

The book will consist of my personal reflections and testimonies as I lived them during the last eighteen years: the genocidal blockade, the 2009 massacre, the 2012 onslaught, the 2014 fifty-one days of constant Israeli attacks, the Great March of Return, the ongoing genocide, and the way forward. Those years have, undoubtedly, played a crucial role in the formation of the Palestinian question and the fate of 2.3 million residents of Gaza, in general, and my own personal consciousness, in particular.

Gaza 2009

TWENTY-TWO DAYS

January 22, 2009

SHARPEVILLE 1960, GAZA 2009

"Where can I bring him a father from? Where can I bring him a mother from? You tell me!"*

These are the desperate words of Subhi Samouni to Al Jazeera's Gaza correspondent. Subhi lost seventeen members of his immediate family, including the parents of his seven-year-old grandson. Shockingly, even as I write this article, corpses of the Samouni family are still being retrieved from under the rubble—fifteen days after the Israeli occupation forces shelled the two houses. The Israeli army locked 120 members of the family in one house for twelve hours before they shelled it.

Subhi's words echo the harsh reality of all Palestinians in Gaza: alone, abandoned, hunted down, brutalized, and, like Subhi's grandson, orphaned. Twenty-two days of savage butchery took the lives of more than 1,300 Palestinians, at least 85 percent of them civilians, including 434 children, 104 women, 16 medics, 4 journalists, 5 foreigners, and 105 elderly people.

What can one say to comfort a man who has the harrowing task of having to bury his entire family, including his wife, his sons, his daughters, and his grandchildren? Tell us and we will relay your words to Uncle Subhi because his loss has made our words of condolences meaningless to our ears.

Think also of words you want to say to seventy-year-old Rashid Muhammad, whose forty-four-year-old son Samir was executed with a single bullet to the heart in front of his wife and children. The Israeli army refused to let an ambulance pick up his corpse for eleven days, so his family had to wait for the assault to stop before they could bury him. Rashid had the excruciatingly painful experience of looking at, touching, kissing, and then burying the

* Originally published in a slightly different form in Haidar Eid, "Sharpeville 1960, Gaza 2009," *Electronic Intifada*, January 22, 2009, electronicintifada.net. Reprinted with permission from the publisher.

decomposed body of his son. Tell this family how to make sense of their harsh reality—say something to make the children sleep, to ease the anguish in the father's heart, to help the wife understand why her husband had to be taken from her.

You might prefer to talk to fourteen-year-old Amira Qirm, whose house in Gaza City was shelled with artillery and phosphorous bombs—bombs that burned to death three members of her immediate family: her father, her twelve-year-old brother, Alaa, and her eleven-year-old sister, Ismat. Alone, injured, and terrified, Amira crawled five hundred metres on her knees to a house close by—it was empty because the family had fled when the Israeli attack began. She stayed there for four days, surviving only on water and listening to the sounds of the Israeli killing machine all around her, too afraid to cry out in pain in case the soldiers heard her. When the owner of the house returned to get clothes for his family, he found Amira, weak and close to death. She is now being treated for her injuries in the overcrowded and under-resourced Al-Shifa Hospital.

You can try to comfort ten-year-old Muhammad Samouni who was found lying next to the bodies of his mother and siblings, five days after they were killed. He would tell you what he has been telling everyone—that his brother woke suddenly after being asleep for a long time. His brother told him that he was hungry, asked for a tomato to eat and then died. Are there any other ten-year-olds in the world who are asked to carry this experience around with them for the rest of their lives? Of course not—this "privilege" is reserved just for Palestinian children because they were born on the land that Israel wants for itself. But it is these traumatized children who will deny Israel what it wants because their very survival is a challenge to that apartheid state. It is these same children who will surely inherit Palestine: it is their birthright and no assault can change that fact—not today, not ever.

And through it all we were subjected to Tzipi Livni, Israel's foreign minister, adamant in her defence of the world's most "moral" army. "We don't target civilians," she lied. "We don't want the Palestinians to leave Gaza. We just want them to move within Gaza itself!" Israeli Prime Minister Ehud Olmert too had something to say to Palestinians in Gaza: "We are not your enemy. Hamas is your enemy."

Amira, Muhammad, Rashid, Subhi, and the more than forty thousand families whose houses have been demolished know differently. Those people who rushed to the cemetery after it was bombed and found the body parts of their dead relatives exposed to the elements know differently. They know that they were deliberately targeted because they are Palestinian. All the rest is propaganda to appease the conscience of those with Palestinian blood on their hands—those who are both inside and outside Israel.

For twenty-two long days and dark nights, Palestinians in Gaza were left alone to face one of the strongest armies in the world—an army that has hundreds of nuclear warheads, thousands of trigger-happy soldiers armed with Merkava tanks, F-16s, Apache helicopters, naval gunships, and phosphorous bombs. Twenty-two sleepless nights, 528 hours of constant shelling and shooting, every single minute expecting to be the next victim.

During these twenty-two days, while morgues overflowed and hospitals struggled to treat the injured, Arab regimes issued tons of statements, condemned and denounced and held one meaningless press conference after another. They even held two summits, the first one convened nineteen full days after the assault on Gaza began and the second one the day after Israel had declared a unilateral ceasefire!

The official Arab position vis-à-vis the Palestinians since 1948, with the exception of the progressive nationalist era (1954–1970), has been a lethal cocktail of cowardice and hypocrisy. Their latest collective failure to break the two-year old Israeli siege of the Gaza Strip and their lack of action to support Palestinians under brutal military assault must be questioned.

Arabs must demand answers from the ineffective Arab League because there was no brotherly solidarity shown to Gazans during the Israeli assault. There was no pan-Arabism evident in their platitudes. Some, shockingly, even found it an appropriate time to blame Palestinians for the situation they found themselves in, instead of demanding that Israel stop its merciless assault.

In Gaza today, we wonder how the expressions of support for

us in the streets of Arab capitals can be translated into action in the absence of democracy. We wonder whether Arab citizens of despotic regimes can nonviolently change the system. We torment ourselves with trying to discern the means that are currently available for democratic political change. With the ongoing massacre in Gaza, and the construction of an apartheid system in Palestine (in all of historic Palestine, including the areas occupied by Israel in 1967), we know that to survive, we must have the support and solidarity of our Arab brothers and sisters. We saw the Arab people rise to that challenge and stand by us for twenty-two days, but we did not see their leaders behind them.

Archbishop Desmond Tutu of South Africa said, "If you are neutral in situations of injustice, you have chosen the side of the oppressor." The UN, EU, Arab League, and the international community by and large have remained silent in the face of atrocities committed by apartheid Israel. They are therefore on the side of Israel. Hundreds of dead corpses of children and women have failed to convince them to act. This is what every Palestinian knows today—whether on the streets of the Gaza Strip, the West Bank, or refugee camps in the Diaspora.

We are, therefore, left with one option; an option that does not wait for the United Nations Security Council, Arab Summits, or Organization of Islamic Conference to convene: the option of people's power. This remains the only power capable of counteracting the massive power imbalance in the Israeli-Palestinian conflict.

The horror of the racist apartheid regime in South Africa was challenged with a sustained campaign of boycott, divestment, and sanctions initiated in 1958 and given new urgency in 1960 after the Sharpeville Massacre. This campaign led ultimately to the collapse of white rule in 1994 and the establishment of a multiracial, democratic state.

Similarly, the Palestinian call for boycott, divestment, and sanctions has been gathering momentum since 2005. Gaza 2009, like Sharpeville 1960, cannot be ignored: it demands a response from all who believe in a common humanity. Now is the time to boycott the apartheid Israeli state, to divest, and to impose sanctions against it. This is the only way to ensure the creation of a secular, democratic state for all in historic Palestine.

This is the only answer to Uncle Subhi's puzzling questions: it is the only way to give his grandson a future, a life of dignity and equality, a life with both peace and justice, because like all children, he deserves nothing less.

February 11, 2009

CULTURE OF RESISTANCE VS. DEFEAT

The ongoing bloodletting in the Gaza Strip and the ability of the Palestinian people to creatively resist the might of the world's fourth strongest army is being hotly debated by Palestinian political forces.* The latest genocidal war, which lasted twenty-two days and in which apartheid Israel used F-16s, Apache helicopters, Merkava tanks, and conventional and nonconventional weapons against the population, has raised many serious questions about the concept of resistance and whether the outcome of the war can, or cannot, be considered a victory for the Palestinian people. The same kind of questions were raised in 2006 when apartheid Israel launched its war against the Lebanese people and brutally killed more than twelve hundred Lebanese.

At the beginning of the Gaza war, we were told by certain sectors of the Palestinian political leadership that "the two sides are to blame: Hamas and Israel" and that "Hamas must stop the launching of the rockets from Gaza." Resistance in all its forms, violent and otherwise, was considered, by these same people, "futile." Now that there are fewer bombs raining down on Gaza, the conflict focuses on whether the outcome of the war was one of victory or defeat. For the Israeli ruling class the answer is clear—in spite of the fact that none of the objectives announced at the beginning of the war have been achieved. It is clear because they, like the defeatist Palestinian camp, simply use the numbers of martyrs, disabled, and homeless to determine victory and defeat.

This approach fails to acknowledge that none of the "objectives" of the war have been achieved: Hamas is still in power, rockets are still being launched, no pro-Oslo† forces have been

* Originally published in a slightly different form in Haidar Eid, "Gaza 2009: Culture of Resistance vs. Defeat," *Electronic Intifada*, February 11, 2009, electronicintifada.net. Reprinted with permission from the publisher.

† The Oslo Accords are two agreements between Israel and the Palestine Liberation Organization (PLO) signed in 1993 and 1995. Despite being touted as

reinstated in the Gaza Strip. The question now being raised by some Palestinian intellectuals and political forces, after the (un) expected brutality of the Israeli occupation forces, is "was it worth it?" The "it" here remains ambiguous depending on the reaction of the listener/reader. What is of interest here is the radical change that some national forces, especially the Left and their intellectuals, have gone through in their mechanical, as opposed to dialectical, interpretation of history and their role, thereafter, in its making.

The war on Gaza has emerged as a political tsunami that has not only put an end to the fiction of the two-state solution and brought liberation rather than independence back to the agenda but has also created a new Palestinian political map given the intellectual debate vis-à-vis the outcome of the war. This new classification of the Palestinian intelligentsia and ruling classes has led to many ex-leftists joining the right-wing anthem of Oslo and its culture of defeatism. Not unlike the Oslo intelligentsia, the new pragmatic Left is characterized by demagogy, opportunism, and shortsightedness. The conduct of these NGOized intellectuals (those emerging from Western-funded "non-governmental organizations"—NGOs) does not show any commitment to their national and historical responsibility.

Michel Foucault's famous formulation, "where there is power, there is resistance," helps us to theorize the political and, hence, the cultural resistance, represented in some of the (post)war discourse.[6] Within the context of resistance, it is worth quoting Frantz Fanon's definitions of the role of the "native intellectual" during the "fighting phase": "The native, after having tried to lose himself in the people and with the people, will . . . shake the people . . . He turns himself into an awakener of the people; hence comes a fighting literature, and a national literature."[7]

On the other hand, there are intellectuals who, according to Fanon's theorization, "give proof that [they have] assimilated the culture of the occupying power. [Their] writings correspond point by point with those of [their] opposite numbers in the mother

---

a peace process, many Palestinians argue that the accords were designed to ensure Israel's continued dominance over the Palestinian people and left many concerns unresolved, including the right of return.

country. [Their] inspiration is European [i.e., Western]."[8] Hence the adoption of the Israeli narrative by some intellectual sections, including NGOized leftists, whereby Israel was exonerated of its crimes: "We are to blame for what happened," "We were not consulted when Hamas started the war!," and "The people are paying the price, not the resistance movement," "Hamas should have renewed the truce," "We cannot afford to lose so many lives; Hamas should have understood this," "There was no resistance at all on the streets of Gaza; resistance men ran away as soon as they saw the first tank."

By the same token, one would also condemn the Algerian, South African, French, Vietnamese, Lebanese, and Egyptian resistance to occupation. The same logic was used by the Bantustan chiefs of South Africa against the anti-apartheid movement; by the Vichy government of France, the South Vietnamese government, the reactionary Egyptian Forces against the progressive regime of Gamal Abdel Nasser in 1956; and even by the Siniora-Jumblatt-Geagea-Hariri March 14 coalition in Lebanon in 2006.

Obviously, these intellectuals' assimilation of the Western mentality, through a process of NGOization, and hence Osloization, makes them look down upon the culture of resistance as useless, futile, and hopeless. Resistance, broadly speaking, is not only the ability to fight back against a militarily more powerful enemy, but also an ability to creatively resist the occupation of one's land. The Oslo defeatists and the neo-Left camp fail to use people power creatively or even to see that it exists. They are defeated because they want to fight the battle on Israel's terms—through the adoption of an Israel-Hamas dichotomy rather than apartheid Israel vs. the Palestinian people—instead of looking at their strengths: that they are the natives of the land, they have international law supporting their claims, they have the moral high ground, the support of international civil society, etc.

One good lesson from the South African struggle is the way it tried to define resistance and its adoption of what it referred to as "the four pillars of the struggle" to achieve victory over the apartheid regime: armed struggle, internal mass mobilization, international solidarity, and the political underground. Alas, none of these pillars seem to fit within the paradigm of the Palestinian neo-Left.

The principled critical legacy of the likes of Ghassan Kanafani, Edward Said, and Frantz Fanon is no longer the guiding torch of the NGOized Left—the secular democratic Left that is supposed to be, as Said would argue, "someone who cannot easily be co-opted by governments or corporations [or donors], and whose *raison d'etre* is to represent all those people and issues that are routinely forgotten or swept under the rug."[9] A fascinating, and timely, remark by Hungarian philosopher György Lukács points to the way the NGOized Left should be talking right now: "When the intellectual's society reaches a historical crossroads in its fight for a clear definition of its identity, the intellectual should be involved in the whole sociopolitical process and leave his ivory tower."

Decolonizing cultural resistance insists on the right to view Palestinian history as a holistic entity, both coherent and integral. It also reflects a national and historical consciousness that Palestinians are able to be agents of change in their present and future regardless of the agendas of Western donors, the Quartet (Russia, the United States, the United Nations, and the European Union), and other official "international" bodies. Yet we see that the neo-democrats of Palestine are unable to acknowledge Palestinian agency because they refuse to respect the will of the people as expressed through the ballot box. This position is meant to synergize with that of their donors and international bodies, who have worked hard over the last two years to delegitimize Palestinian agency.

This lack of political consciousness and the search for individual solutions—the major characteristics of defeatist ideology—contradict the collective national reality of the colonized Palestinians. Political consciousness must begin with a rejection of the conditions imposed by the Israeli occupation and the Quartet on the majority of Palestinians and even more crucially, a rejection of the crumbs that are offered as a reward for good behaviour to a select minority of Palestinians. Indeed, class consciousness is dialectically related to the struggle for national liberation. It is the interests of some NGOized groups, ex-leftists, and neoliberals, whose defeatist perspective on the outcome of Gaza 2009 is being disseminated with the help of some unpopular media outlets, that is at stake here—not the interests of the Palestinian people, who have gained even more legitimacy through their steadfast resistance to the Israeli bombardment.

Osloized and NGOized classes argue that the only solution to the Israeli-Palestine conflict is the establishment of two states, which basically means the creation of an independent Palestine on 22 percent of Mandate Palestine. They maintain that the only way to reach independence is through negotiations, though more than ten years of negotiations have not moved the Israeli position at all. The establishment of a Palestinian state is not mentioned in any of the clauses of the Oslo agreement, thus leaving the matter to be determined by the balance of power in the region. This balance tilts in favour of Israel, which rejects the establishment of a sovereign Palestinian state, in spite of its recognition of the Palestinian people and its national movement, the Palestine Liberation Organization (PLO). No Israeli party, neither Labor, Likud, nor Kadima is ready to accept a Palestinian state as the expression of the right of the Palestinian people to self-determination. The impasse negotiations have reached has proven the oppositional camp correct.

Hence the "shocking" results of the 2006 elections, in which Hamas won the majority of the seats of the Palestinian Legislative Council. Both liberals and leftists were "surprised" and even felt "betrayed!" Accusations of the "immaturity" and even "backwardness" of the Palestinian people have been thrown around since then. Nothing was mentioned about the failure of "the peace process," nor the end of the two-state solution and, thereafter, the necessity and need for a new national program that can mobilize the masses; a program that is necessarily democratic in its nature; one that respects resistance in its different forms and, ultimately, guarantees *peace with justice.*

It is this lack of a political vision and a clear-cut ideological program that allows for the contortions of the Osloized classes. It is this lack that makes it prepared to recognize a "Jewish state" alongside a Palestinian state, including the legitimization of discriminatory practices applied by Israel against its non-Jewish—that is, mainly Palestinian citizens and residents—since 1948, and the end of the right of return of more than six million refugees. What we are constantly told is either accept Israeli occupation in its ugliest form—that is, the ongoing presence of the apartheid wall, colonies, checkpoints, zigzag roads, colour-coded number plates, house demolitions, and security coordination supervised by a retired American general—or have a hermetic medieval siege imposed on us, but still die with dignity. The first option seems to be the favourite of some NGOized "activists."

The new, much-needed program, however, must make the necessary link between all Palestinian struggles: the occupation of Gaza and the West Bank, Israel's ethnically-based discrimination and rights violations of more than one million Palestinian citizens, and the 1948 externally displaced refugees. Gaza 2009 was not a defeat but a victory because in Gaza the Israelis shot the two-state solution in the head; it is a victory achieved with the blood of those children, men, and women who sacrificed their lives so that we could live and continue to resist, not surrender. Those Palestinians that are mourning the demise of the two-prison solution are out of step with new facts on the ground: there can be no going back to fake solutions and negotiations; it is time for a final push to real freedom and statehood. They can join other Palestinians, and internationals, in their demand for a secular, democratic state in Mandate Palestine with equality for all or they can walk into the dustbin of history.

November 19, 2009

FROM GAZA TO OBAMA

An Open Letter

Dear Mr. President,
You will probably not read this letter due to your busy schedule and the huge number of messages you receive from presidents, kings, princes, sheiks, and prime ministers.* Who is a Palestinian academic from Gaza, after all, to have the guts and write an open letter to the president of the United States of America?

What has triggered this letter is a picture of your excellency sitting with the late Palestinian intellectual Edward Said. That, of course, happened before 2004—that is, before you underwent a process of metamorphosis that I personally think is unprecedented in history. Seeing you with Edward Said, I must say, surprised me. Said, a true public intellectual, must have said something to you about the suffering of the Palestinian people. In the picture, you and your wife seem to be listening attentively, and admiringly, to him. But the point remains: Did you *really* understand his eloquent, passionate defence of the rights of the indigenous inhabitants of Palestine? Judging from your recent policy shifts, I very much doubt it. It is precisely the incongruity between the photograph and these policy shifts that has prompted this letter.

Mr. President,
The whole world celebrated your election as the first African American president of the US. I did not. Neither did the inhabitants of the concentration camp where I live. Your sympathetic visit to Sderot—an Israeli town that was the Palestinian village of Najd until 1948 when its people were ethnically cleansed—three years

* Originally published in a slightly different form in Haidar Eid, "An Open Letter to Barack Obama," SocialistWorker.org, November 19, 2009, socialistworker.org. Reprinted with permission from the publisher.

after your first visit to a Kibbutz in northern Israel in support of its residents, and after your pledge to be committed to the security of the state of Israel and its "right" to retain unified Jerusalem as the capital city of the Jewish people—to give but few examples—were all clear indications of where your heart lies.

Another reason for the writing of this letter is shock at the indifference and arrogance with which Secretary of State Hillary Clinton dismissed Palestinian concerns about Israel's illegal Jewish-only settlements in the West Bank. Only a few weeks ago you made the admirable statement that all Jewish settlement must halt, and you made it clear that this included expansion of existing settlements as well as the construction of new settlements. However, when Netanyahu let it be known that he had no intention of stopping settlements, you missed a historic opportunity to draw a line: no more billions and no more weapons for Israel unless and until this condition is met. Now Clinton has the Herculean task of pretending that your position on Jewish settlements has not changed, although it is clear you have chosen not to use the very real power at your disposal to bring Israeli policy into line.

About six months after your election, you gave a speech in Cairo, addressed to the Arab and Islamic worlds, that some people found impressive. I found it impressive in form but not in substance because your actions have not matched your rhetoric. Why did I not buy the new language of the new American administration? Because while you were giving your speech, we were burying my neighbour, a terminally ill patient who needed treatment in a hospital abroad since, thanks to the siege imposed by your own administration and Israel on the Gaza Strip, the facilities that would have saved his life are not available in Gaza. Like more than four hundred terminally ill people in Gaza, my neighbour lost his life. In spite of the fine Arabic words of peace, "salaam aleikum," you made it crystal clear that the point of reference in any negotiations in the Israeli-Palestinian conflict is Israel's security. By doing that, Mr. President, you are effectively marginalizing the whole issue of Palestine and unfortunately setting the stage for renewed Israeli assaults against a starving Gaza, an entity that has, thanks to your "unbreakable" ties with Israel, been transformed into the largest concentration camp on earth.

Your failure to support the Goldstone Report, your indifference, not to say your contribution, to Palestinian suffering and the process of "politicide" against the Palestinian people of Gaza is unfathomable, to say the least, coming from a man who listened so earnestly to Edward Said. Your advisers must have told you about the cutting off of medicine, food, and fuel to the concentration camp where I live. Patients in need of dialysis and other urgent medical treatment are dying every single day. A majority of our children, many the same age as your two beautiful daughters, are badly undernourished.

You must have skimmed through the executive summary of the Goldstone Report detailing the horror inflicted on 1.5 million civilians for twenty-two days, horror caused by F-16s, Apache helicopters, and phosphorus bombs made in American factories. Hundreds of children were burned to death by phosphorus bombs; pregnant women were brutally targeted in what Israeli soldiers boasted of on their T-Shirts: "One bullet, Two kills." And yet, not a single word of sympathy, Mr. President! Edward Said had this to say upon his first visit to Gaza: "It's the most terrifying place I've ever been in . . . it's a horrifyingly sad place because of the desperation and misery of the way people live. I was unprepared for camps that are much worse than anything I saw in South Africa." This was back in 1993, Mr. President, before conditions dramatically deteriorated. Gaza has now become, as the leading Israeli human rights organization B'Tselem describes it, "the largest prison on earth."

Mr. Obama,
Unlike your predecessor, you seem to be a smart man. You must have realized that a two-state solution has been rendered impossible by Israeli colonization of the West Bank, by the war on Gaza, by the construction of the apartheid wall, by the expansion of so-called Greater Jerusalem, and by the increase in the number of Jewish settlers in the West Bank. You must have realized also that there are six million refugees, most of whom live in miserable conditions waiting for courageous, visionary leaders committed to true democracy, human rights, and international law to implement UN Resolution 194. And yet, you and your secretary of state, like every US president since 1967, have decided to support Israel in

creating conditions that made the two-state solution impossible, impractical, and unjust.

Were you a supporter of the Bantustan system in South Africa under the apartheid system? Are you opposed to equal rights and the transformation of Israel/Palestine into a state for all its citizens? The two-state solution means the Bantustanization of Palestine, a solution you, to our knowledge, never supported for South Africa. Are you, Mr. President, opposed to civic democracy, which is the demand of most Palestinian civil society and grassroots organizations? This is what your role models, Martin Luther King Jr. and Steve Biko, died for. Was Nelson Mandela wrong to spend twenty-seven years of his life in pursuit of justice by demanding equality for the indigenous people of South Africa? Do you realize that what you are supporting in the Middle East is a racist solution par excellence? A solution based on ethnic nationalism. Your secretary of state and envoy to the Middle East, unashamedly, stood with beaming smiles next to Israeli Foreign Minister Avigdor Lieberman, who not only openly defends the ethnic cleansing of Palestinians but also calls for a new genocide in Gaza. Do you realize, Mr. President, that this Hitlerite fascist might become Israel's next prime minister, thanks to your administration's complacency and support?

Our only immediate demand is that your administration ensures that Israel fulfills its obligations in terms of international law. Is that too much to ask?

Mr. President Barack Hussein Obama,
We, the Palestinian people, are fed up!

Sincerely,
Professor Haidar Eid
Gaza, Palestine

July 27, 2010

THE ENDURING SIEGE

Israeli Apartheid in Gaza?

The Palestinian national movement has overlooked this question: Does the Gaza Strip resemble the racist Bantustans of apartheid South Africa?* During the apartheid era, South Africa's Black population was kept in isolation and without political and civil rights. Is Gaza similar? The answer is yes and no.

What is apartheid? As defined by the 1973 United Nations convention, apartheid is a policy of racial or ethnic segregation founded on a set of discriminatory practices that favour a specific group in order to ensure its racial supremacy over another group.[10] In Israel, institutionalized racial discrimination is unequivocally founded on ensuring the primacy of a group of Jewish settlers over the Palestinian Arabs. When comparing the applications of the apartheid policy, it is difficult to identify any differences between white rule in South Africa and its Israeli counterpart in Palestine in terms of the segregation and designation of certain areas to Israeli Jews and others to the Arabs, the delineation of certain laws and privileges for Jews, and a discriminatory set of laws that apply only to Palestinians.

Currently, in both Israel and the Occupied Palestinian Territories (OPT) there are two road systems, two housing systems, two educational systems, and different legal and administrative systems for Jews and non-Jews. Every law enacted during the South African apartheid system has a corresponding law in Israel. This includes the Group Areas Act, the Prohibition of Mixed Marriages Act, the Law on Movement and Permits, the Public Safety Act, the Population Registration Act, the Immorality Act, the Land Act, and, of course, the Bantu Homelands Citizenship

* Originally published in a slightly different form in Haidar Eid, "Gaza: The Enduring Siege," *Al-Shabaka*, July 27, 2010, al-shabaka.org. Reprinted with permission from the publisher.

Act. The corresponding Israeli laws are the Law of Return, the 2003 "temporary" laws prohibiting mixed marriages, the Population Registry Law, the Citizenship and Entry into Israel Law, the Israeli Nationality Law, and land and property laws.

Like South Africa, Israel's brand of apartheid is mixed with settler colonialism. As in the United States, Australia, New Zealand, and Canada, settler colonialism in Israel and South Africa has also involved the ethnic cleansing or genocide of the indigenous people influenced by a racist and/or religious ideology of supremacy.

When evaluated along these lines, the term apartheid clearly applies to Israeli policies in the Gaza Strip. The Palestinians of the Gaza Strip are isolated from the rest of the population in historical Palestine and do not enjoy minimum political rights and basic living conditions available to Jewish residents because they were born to mothers from the "wrong" religion. In this context, it should be recalled that 80 percent of the population in the Strip were ethnically cleansed in 1948 and are barred from returning to the villages and cities from which they were driven.

The Bantustans were part of the apartheid regime's racist formula to separate the Black population and preserve "white supremacy." Although the Bantustans were called "independent homelands," their inhabitants were not granted equal rights or even independent political decision-making power—a harbinger of what is planned for the so-called independent Palestinian state within the June 1967 borders. In South Africa, the debate was about eleven states that could live side by side in peace. In spite of Pretoria's best efforts, the Bantustans gained no international recognition save from Israel.

Gaza is deprived of even this racist formula. Israel appears to have learned a lesson from South Africa. It did not appoint local leaders to provide "limited self-government" over the West Bank and Gaza. Rather, in coordination with the United States and shielded by the international community, Israel allowed "free" elections to take place so that the Bantustanization process could gain "legitimacy" and international approval with the consent of the indigenous people. Although hailed internationally, the elections that took place under occupation were a Palestinian tragedy. Israel succeeded in enticing the indigenous people in Palestine to promote the illusion of potential "independence" for segments of 22 percent of historical Palestine. These parcels of land without sovereignty would be sold to the world as an independent Palestinian state.

Gaza Under Siege

At the same time, the answer to the question of whether "apartheid" applies to Gaza is also no. Between the Oslo Accord years (1993–2002), the Gaza Strip has devolved from a Bantustan into a large concentration camp. Several South African anti-apartheid activists, including Nobel Peace Prize winner Archbishop Desmond Tutu, said during their visits to the OPT that what they saw was far worse than what South Africans witnessed during apartheid. The difference between the two kindred regimes—Israel and apartheid South Africa—is the difference between inferiority and dehumanization. As Saree Makdisi has explained, it is a difference between exploitation and genocide.[11]

Never, throughout the history of apartheid in South Africa, did racist forces use the full force of their military against the civilian population in townships. In contrast, since the outbreak of the second Palestinian Intifada in September 2000 and culminating in the 2008–2009 winter invasion, Gaza has been attacked by F-16s, Apache helicopter gunships, warships, Merkava Tanks, and internationally prohibited phosphorus bombs.

Israel's siege on Gaza was imposed after Palestinians elected Hamas in internationally sanctioned and observed elections in 2006. It was tightened after Hamas defeated forces loyal to the Fatah faction of Palestinian Authority President Mahmoud Abbas in June 2007. Since then, the list of items banned from entering Gaza has covered more than two hundred articles, including cement, paper, cancer medications, and even pasta and chocolate! According to the Israeli organization Gisha: Legal Center for Freedom of Movement, Israel granted access to only ninety-seven articles, compared to four thousand before the blockade. About 80 percent of the Gaza Strip's population survive on humanitarian aid. More than 90 percent of Gaza's factories have been shut down.

When the eighteen-month old siege was unable to break the will of Palestinians in Gaza, Israel launched its deadly invasion at the end of 2008. According to the human rights organizations and the UN sanctioned Goldstone Report, over fourteen hundred Palestinians, including over three hundred children, were killed and thousands wounded. Israel destroyed at least 11,000 homes, 105 factories, 20 hospitals and clinics, as well as 159 schools, universities, and technical institutes. Furthermore, it resulted in the displacement of 51,800 persons of whom 20,000 remain homeless.

Commenting on this situation, Karen Abu Zayd, former commissioner-general for the United Nations Relief and Works Agency for Palestine Refugees in the Near East (UNWRA) said: "Gaza is on the threshold of becoming the first territory to be intentionally reduced to a state of abject destitution with the knowledge, acquiescence, and—some would say—encouragement of the international community."

Gaza 2012

HISTORY REPEATS ITSELF

November 20, 2012

GAZA 2012!

It looks like history is repeating itself!* We are in the month of December, 2008. But some ugly masks have been changed. Instead of Ehud Olmert, we have Benjamin Netanyahu, and instead of Tzipi Livni shaking her finger in Cairo and threatening the innocent people of Gaza, beside dictator Hosni Mubarak's minister of foreign affairs we have the fascist minister Avigdor Lieberman vowing to "transfer" or "nuke" us!

And here, in Gaza, we see the angelic faces of seven-year-old Ranan Arafat, and eleven-month-old Omar al-Mashharawi, in the arms of his father, coming out of the morgue of Al-Shifa Hospital.

As if time has decided to stand still! Gaza 2012 is Gaza 2009!

But Mubarak has gone. And so has his Foreign Affairs Minister Ahmed Abu el-Gheit, with his threats to break the legs of our children, who, according to him, posed "a threat" to Egypt's national security. The Arab Spring came as an expression of a strong, popular desire to get rid of such corrupt, dictatorial, puppet regimes.

So what do we, Palestinians, expect from the new Egypt? Egypt, which accepted, as part of the Mubarak legacy, to act as a mediator between "the two sides." And by doing so, it swallowed the bait and convinced the Palestinian resistance factions, last week, to abide by a truce that Israel used as a cover to assassinate a senior Palestinian commander it had been trying to kill for several years.[12]

What was the Egyptian reaction to this Israeli manipulation?

The decision to recall the Egyptian ambassador from Tel Aviv is a welcome step, but it should be the beginning of further steps to reconsider all the agreements signed with Israel, especially the Camp David Accords (1978).† Gaza, after all, is an integral part

* Originally published in a slightly different form in Haidar Eid, "Gaza 2012!" Opinion, *Al-Jazeera*, November 19, 2012, aljazeera.com. Reprinted with permission from the publisher.

† The Camp David Accords were two agreements signed in 1978 by Egypt and Israel with the support of the US. The intention of the Accords was to broker peace

of Egypt's national security. We expect Egypt to lead an Arab campaign to isolate apartheid Israel until it complies with international law.

Palestinian deterrence depends on the fact that we have what the late Edward Said called "the higher moral ground," and our victory at the end will be the inevitable result of our steadfastness that has not wavered despite the feeling that we are left on our own. When Israel attacked Gaza, for twenty-two consecutive days in 2009, it made it crystal clear that it had four objectives that, unsurprisingly, it failed to achieve. Now, in 2012, Israel has declared "new" objectives for its new barbaric war on the children and women of Gaza. But the residents of Gaza are resilient and steadfast, which gives them the right, together with rest of the Palestinian people in the Diaspora, the West Bank, and 1948, to steer the international campaign to boycott apartheid Israel. But that requires the full support of the new Arab world. Our only demand, at this point in time, is a boycott of Israel economically, politically, and culturally. This is the least the indifferent "international community" can do to make up for its complicity in the crimes committed by apartheid Israel against our people.

Israel has tested the water of the Arab Spring since its inception. Had it not been for the complicity of the reactionary Arab regimes and the international conspiracy of silence, apartheid Israel would not have attacked Gaza. PERIOD. In 2009, Palestinians of Gaza were left alone to face an army equipped with F-16 aircraft and Apache and phosphorus bombs. Not only that, but fingers were pointed at us. Now is the moment of truth, the moment of sending a clear message from the new Arab world: the time of Mubarak and Abu el-Gheit is gone. That the power of deterrence, in light of the massive imbalance of power between Israel and the Palestinians, lies with the ordinary citizen in the streets of Tunis, Cairo, Rabat, Doha, Amman, and Muscat. The demonstrations that have erupted

---

between Israel and the Arab countries. One of the agreements dealt with the Palestinian territories but was written without Palestinian participation and was condemned by the United Nations. The Accords promised the withdrawal of Israeli troops from the West Bank and Gaza after the election of a self-governing authority but denied the right of Palestinians to have a Palestinian state. It made no mention of the right to return or the status of Jerusalem.

in London, New York, Glasgow, and other cities must be translated into a new, concrete reality steered by Palestinians and Arabs. Egyptians, in particular, are partners, not mediators.

As for the Palestinians, we must unify our ranks on the ground in a national front, a front that will turn its back on the remnants of the ugly Oslo days and security coordination, one that declares its divorce from all racist proposals. And we must make it absolutely clear that there is no place for normalizers among us from now on. *Khalaas*. We will chase all normalizers with the blood of our children! We will not allow them to sit with us from now on until they sever their relations with the occupation and stop whitewashing its ugly face; a face that is stained with the blood of Palestinian children, Omar Mashharawi, Ranan Arafat, Safaa Hammoudeh, Mohamed Dardouna, and the Samouni children.

Gaza 2009 was the Sharpeville and Guernica of Palestine. Gaza 2012 is Palestine's Soweto 1976, leading inexorably to implementation of the right of return and the end of ALL racist solutions; the beginning of the end of occupation, colonization, and apartheid in Palestine.

Let history repeat itself, but not as a tragedy this time: 1976 witnessed the beginning of the end of apartheid in South Africa; 2012 will be the turning point that will lead to the end of apartheid in Palestine.

May 28, 2013

PERSONAL REFLECTIONS ON THE NAKBA

We shall meet awhile
After a year
After two years
And generation . . .
. . .
And we were rejuvenated, Death and I,
In your first front
And in window of your house.
Death and I are two faces-
Why now do you flee from my face,
Why now do you flee?
Why now do you flee from
What makes wheat the earth's eyelashes, from
What makes the volcano another face to jasmine?
Why now do you flee?
. . .
I sip kisses
From the blade of knives.
Come, let's join the massacre!
. . .
I am he in whose skin
The shackles etch
A likeness of the homeland
—Mahmoud Darwish, "Birds Die in Galilee"

May 2005; my mother, Amneh Abdullah Ahmed Eid, made the decision that she could no longer endure her ongoing Nakba.* Was it a coincidence—though I hardly believe in such

* Originally published in a slightly different form in Haidar Eid, "Personal Reflections on the Nakba," *Mondoweiss*, May 28, 2013, mondoweiss.net. Reprinted with permission from the publisher.

coincidences—that she, with the rest of the Eid clan, was forced out of her paradise, Zarnouqa, in May 1948, fifty-seven years earlier? She had been only nineteen then, with a baby who she would lose two years later.

Am I being sentimental?!

What do I know about Zarnouqa? What is it that connects me to that "forgotten," destroyed village turned into an industrial zone? When I decided to post Amneh's photo on my Facebook page, I wrote "Zarnouqa" under it! Why?

Ben Gurion thought I would "forget" after Amneh died. But as Edward Said said so eloquently: "Every Palestinian knows perfectly well that what has happened to us over the last six decades is a direct consequence of Israel's destruction of our society in 1948 . . . The problem is that a clear, direct line from our misfortunes in 1948 to our misfortunes in the present cannot be drawn, thanks to the complexity of our experience."[13]

Why is it that even though I was born sixteen years after the Nakba, I have these recurring nightmares—the same nightmares as Naji al-Ali used to have? A nightmare of hundreds of thousands of people, including my parents, being forced out of their homes en masse! Mother, wearing a *thoub*,* carrying a child, but looking backward. I am there, but not there. And I wake up sweating. Carl Jung would have called it an archetype from the "Palestinian Collective Unconscious."

The day Amneh died, she opened her eyes to ask whether my father had returned from Jaffa. She had made a decision to erase fifty-seven years of dispossession, regardless.

The day she died, I wrote this:

Olive Trees Do Not Die.
Is there a sky without birds?
Is there a life without a promised land?
Is there (a) Palestine without (a) Zarnouqa?
And is there (an) Amneh without (a) Hafez?

* Palestinian dress

No. Amneh Abdullah Eid, born in 1929 in the village of Zarnouqa, had decided not to put up with Israel any more.

From Zarnouqa to Deir el Balah, from Deir el Balah to Gaza City, from Gaza to Nuseirat refugee camp and back to Gaza and to Nuseirat again, where the birds stopped flying, where she lost the only Man she had known for more than sixty years. For fifty-seven years she had been waiting, with him—her Man, the *Si Sayyed* of her life, the "light of her eyes," the Palestine of her heart, the Zalameh of her family,* the Nasser of her "political" world—to return.

Four months ago, Hafez Abdulhafez Eid, also born in the village of Zarnouqa, had his appointment with the "birdless" sky. He fixed his wings, forgot to say goodbye, and took off. From his flat, surrounded by his granddaughters, Abu† Marwan, as he was known in the densely populated camp, could not bear the emptiness of the sky any more. For fifty-seven years (minus four months), he had been away from Zarnouqa, and his big heart was tired; all brothers had already set sail, three sons had left prematurely, and Umm‡ Marwan had been bed-ridden for seven years. What is a (wo)man's heart? Where can it take you? It can take you to the sky; to your promised land: to *Zarnouqa*.

But Hajjeh§ Um Marwan insisted that the fifty-seventh anniversary of the Nakba take place without him. "Let Israel celebrate its birthday tomorrow. I am flying back to Zarnouqa today. Zalamaty¶ cannot fly alone in the empty sky." Over the last ten years she lost two sons, besides the child she had lost three years after the Nakba, suffered two massive strokes, fought gangrene and won the battle, and lost Zalametha.** And missed me!

Wing in wing, Hafez and Amneh Eid are flying back to their promised land.

* the "man of her family"

† Father

‡ Mother

§ Men and women who perform pilgrimage are called Haj and Hajjeh.

¶ "her man"

** "her man"

Gaza 2014

THE WORLD'S BIGGEST GRAVEYARD

February 18, 2014

THE ALTERNATIVE IS BDS!

As BDS activists, we are no longer interested in the sterile opposition to normalization generated by the Oslo Accords but rather in formulating the kind of response that could actually defeat multiple forms of Zionist oppression: occupation, ethnic cleansing, and apartheid.* The moment the entire international community, civil society, and governments decide to act as it did against the apartheid system of white South Africa, Israel would succumb to the voice of reason represented by the 2005 BDS call issued by more than 170 civil society organizations and endorsed by almost all influential political forces from Right to Left of the political spectrum in historic Palestine and the Diaspora.

Since the world is showing a growing disapproval of Israel's occupation of the West Bank and its settlement policies there, the urgent question now is how long the world will tolerate Israel's blatant constitutional racism.

The latest BDS success triggered by the American Studies Association (ASA) resolution to endorse a boycott of Israeli academic institutions is, in fact, what we have been calling for since 2004, when the Palestinian Campaign for the Academic and Cultural Boycott of Israel was launched. I, as a resident of Gaza and an academic, have been unable to fathom how it is that some reputable universities sign agreements with Israeli universities despite the policy of ethnic cleansing and the latest war crimes committed against the people of Gaza by Israel. Israeli academic institutions are known to be complicit in Israel's policy of colonization and apartheid.

Is it not crystal clear, after all these years and thousands of reports by mainstream human rights organizations, that millions

* Originally published in a slightly different form in Haidar Eid, "The Alternative Is BDS," *Mondoweiss*, February 18, 2014, mondoweiss.net. Reprinted with permission from the publisher.

of Palestinians are denied the full right to education in the OPT and in the refugee camps? Think about it, our education is denied because of more than six hundred Israeli checkpoints, the medieval siege of Gaza, and the apartheid-like discrimination faced by Palestinian students in Israel. We are discriminated against for the simple fact that we were not born to Jewish mothers.

Thousands of Palestinian students and lecturers are in Israeli dungeons, often without trial or sentenced by military courts. All credible international human rights and humanitarian organizations have detailed how the Israeli military deliberately targets Palestinian students and schools, including UN schools. Shouldn't academics and researchers be familiar with those reports?

We believe that it is our right to expect people of conscience, especially academics and students, to join us in our struggle against Israeli apartheid by boycotting this intransigent, racist, and militarized Israeli regime and the institutions that keep it thriving.

ASA members must have found it unconscionable that their association remain complicit in Palestinian oppression by pretending to have "business as usual" with apartheid. We, Palestinians, are an oppressed people without a state. We increasingly rely on international law and solidarity for our very survival.

What we want is the implementation of international law, putting an end to the Israeli military occupation of Arab lands occupied in 1967, fighting against the policy of colonization and apartheid as practised by Israel against the indigenous population of Palestine of 1948, and the return of Palestinian refugees who were ethnically cleaned in 1948. Now, is that a call for the end of the state of Israel? Was the boycott of apartheid meant to end South Africa as a country or to end racism in its ugliest from?

Israel is a settler-colonialist, apartheid state and the methods—or tools of struggle—used against apartheid South Africa can be used as a model in our struggle against apartheid Israel. Transforming Israel from an ethno-religious apartheid state into a democracy should be the objective of every single person believing in liberal democracy in general. But some "liberals" keep whining that one of the "scary aims of BDS" is equal rights and warning that the state of Israel might be in peril if BDS has its way.

With pressure imposed by the international community through a BDS campaign similar to the anti-apartheid campaign that brought apartheid South Africa to an end, we believe that Israel itself can be pressured to end its multitiered system of oppression.

The BDS campaign is intended to lead to satisfying the democratic rights of the Palestinian people in its three components—including of course the Palestinian citizens of the state of Israel who experience Israel's institutional racism first hand. That is why one of the major demands of the BDS campaign, defended by all those who have endorsed the above mentioned BDS call in 2005, is the call for the end of the policy of apartheid practised against the Palestinians of 1948. We strongly believe that the struggles of the Palestinian people whether in 1948 or in 1967, that is to say the West Bank and Gaza Strip, and even in the Diaspora, are inseparable. That is why we think that our alternative, which is rights-based, to Oslo's facade of "peace" based on normalization can provide all Palestinians with a solution that guarantees the right of return and equality for the 1948 inhabitants.

To echo a quote often attributed to Mahatma Ghandi: in 2005 they ignored the BDS call, then they laughed at us, now they are fighting us, and then we will win!

July 12, 2014

SIGNPOSTS ON THE ROAD TO LIBERATION

On my notebooks from school
On my desk and the trees
On the sand on the snow
I write your name
On every page read
On all the white sheets
Stone blood paper or ash
I write your name . . .
Liberty

—Paul Eluard, "Liberty"

Edward Said wrote extensively about the necessity of writing the Palestinian narrative.* But he also argued, rightly, that we were never allowed to do so. Now, we in Gaza have decided to write our narratives, sometimes with blood.

Because they leave a mark on our individual and collective consciousness, we call them martyrs. Those who took up arms or pens—Che Guevara, Ghassan Kanafani, Naji al-Ali, Dalal Mughrabi, Shadia Abu Ghazaleh, Steve Biko, Salavador Allende, Rosa Luxemburg, Patrice Lumumba, to mention but a few—have booked their places there.

But there are others, much younger, unknown to many, who have played a major role in the formation of our consciousness. They visit me every night; I see them in my dreams. I talk to them: I discuss serious issues with them, more serious than any living person can imagine.

At 139 square miles, Gaza is the largest refugee camp on earth, a reminder of the ongoing Nakba. The inhabitants of Gaza have

* Originally published in a slightly different form in Haidar Eid, "Gaza: Signposts on the Road to Liberation," *Electronic Intifada,* July 12, 2014, electronicintifada.net. Reprinted with permission from the publisher.

become the most unwanted Palestinians, the black heart that no one wants to see, the "Negroes" of the American South, the Black natives of apartheid South Africa. The surplus population that the powerful, macho, white Ashkenazi Israeli cannot coexist with.

Landmarks

The years 1987, 2009, 2012, and now 2014 are signposts on the road to our liberation. But they have also been landmarks in the formation of my own consciousness, not unlike those left by the great martyrs mentioned above.

1987: Ashraf Eid, fifteen years old, my cousin's son/sun. One bullet, shot by an Israeli sniper in Rafah, penetrated his small heart. It was the end of a long fasting day during the holy month of Ramadan. One bullet, the end of Ashraf's life, a mark on my consciousness.

2009: Maather Abu Znaid, twenty-four, my student. I was teaching my first course, "The Novel," at Al-Aqsa University in 2005 in Khan Younis. I taught two novels, one by Ghassan Kanafani and, ironically, another by the racist writer and Nobel Laureate V.S. Naipaul. Students know me to be "strict" and "stingy" in giving marks, but Maather got 92 percent, a mark I rarely award. She graduated with high honours—an intelligent student with big, expansive dreams. She wanted to further her studies, but in Gaza, dreams fly away. During the Gaza massacre of 2009, Maather was targeted and hit by a drone missile as she left her house. Her family is still trying to find parts of her body, if they ever can. That was a dream cut short. One drone missile, end of dreams; another mark on my consciousness.

2009: Forty-four-year-old Samir Muhammad was executed with a single bullet to the heart in front of his wife and children. The Israeli army refused to let an ambulance pick up his corpse for eleven days so his family had to wait for the assault to stop before they could bury him. His father, Rashid, told me in agonizing detail how he had the excruciatingly painful experience of looking at, touching, kissing, and then burying the decomposed body of his son. Rashid is originally from my parents' village, Zarnouqa; he knew them well. Samir could have been me. Single bullet: Zarnouqa is not far.

2009: Muhammad Samouni, ten, was found lying next to the bodies of his mother and siblings, five days after they were killed. He would tell you what he has been telling everyone—that his brother woke suddenly after being asleep for a long time. His brother told him that he was hungry, asked for a tomato to eat and then died. A torch in the dark depths of my consciousness.

2009: Ismat, eleven, and Alaa Qirm, twelve, whose house in Gaza City was shelled with artillery and phosphorous bombs—bombs that burned them to death together with their father, leaving behind their fourteen-year-old sister Amira. Alone, injured, and terrified, Amira crawled 500 metres on her knees to a house close by, which happened to be my cousin's home. It was empty because the family had fled when the Israeli attack began. She stayed there for four days, surviving only on water. When my cousin returned to get clothes for his family, he found Amira, weak and close to death. The bodies of her siblings and father were decomposed. Another deep scar left in the depths of my consciousness.

2014: Najla al-Haj, a student at Al-Aqsa University, killed with her family in an Israeli air strike on the home of her family in Khan Younis in southern Gaza. She was talking to her university friends online just a few hours before. Hanadi, another student, as well as my eighteen-year-old niece Shimo, only learned of their friend's death hours later when they awoke for *suhour*, the Ramadan pre-fast meal. Hanadi went immediately to Najla's Facebook page. The last thing Najla wrote was: "God be with us. Oh, hello martyrdom." Najla al-Haj died with seven others from her family. One airstrike, martyrdom of an entire family; a signpost on the road back to Haifa.

Torment

As I argued in 2012 and 2009, the fact that these Palestinians were not born to Jewish mothers is enough reason to deprive them of their right to live equally with the citizens of the state of Israel. Hence, like the Black natives of South Africa, they must be isolated in a Bantustan, in accordance with the terms of the 1993 Oslo Accords. If those corralled into a cage show any resistance to this plan, they must be severely punished—sometimes by a single bullet, sometimes by missiles made in the United States, and sometimes by phosphorus bombs.

How I can contribute to making their deaths a meaningful one is the question that has been tormenting me for years. Being a teacher of resistance literature, two Palestinian novels have also left their mark: Ghassan Kanafani's *Men in the Sun* and *All That is Left to You*.[14] In the former, we, Palestinian refugees, are the weaker party; the passive, hiding victims who dare not bang on the walls of the searingly hot tanker truck in which we are concealed.

But in *All That is Left to You*, Hamid, like me a refugee, is the Palestinian protagonist who chooses to act and become an agent of change. If this brings death, it will be a death that opens up possibilities for a better life to others.

Similarly, the offer that is given to us in Gaza and Palestine today is that we can either have a dignified death as we struggle, or we can continue to live in slavery. Those who left a mark on my consciousness made the former choice and allowed us to live. The Palestinian people, and Gazans in particular, have been living an unending massacre since 1948. We can no longer negotiate about improving the conditions of oppression; it is either the full menu of rights or nothing. And that means the end of occupation, apartheid, and colonialism.

Liberation, Not Coordination

At the end of the massacre of 180 people in November 2012, the vast majority civilians, we were told that the end of the massacre would lead to the lifting of the siege. That did not happen. Now, the lifting of the siege is not enough. When this barbaric attack ends with the victory of the Palestinian people, we do not want a Palestinian Authority, nor Oslo Accords, nor "security coordination."

Like the previous massacres in 2009 and 2012, the current one must become a signpost on our long walk to liberation. Liberation is the antithesis of Oslo and the racist two-state solution. Any revolutionary alternative offered by resistance on the ground must, therefore, divorce itself from all previous agreements.

The end of this genocidal war must necessarily mean the end of Oslo because, simply put, the Oslo Accords are the equivalent of slavery, and there is nothing to lose but our chains and our refugee tents.

Ashraf, Maather, Najla, Ismat, Alaa, Muhammad, and Samir deserve better: they deserve a free country in which their names are signposted on the streets of Haifa, Jaffa, and Zarnouqa.

July 31, 2014

THE RAPE OF GAZA

> The only thing that could deter a suicide bomber is knowing that if caught, his sister or his mother would be raped.
>
> —Mordechai Kedar, Bar-Ilan University

Gaza has gone from being the world's biggest concentration camp to being the world's biggest graveyard. How can one describe the ongoing massacre in Gaza with language that has long been proven to be slippery?*

Where is one to start and finish if one wants a semiological analysis of the dramatic footage of children bleeding to death despite Israel's attempts to convince us that these children were not the targets, the militants were?

If there were any questions to be asked, they would be about the nature of a hegemonic modern ideology that dehumanizes toddlers and drives soldiers to shoot women and shell hospitals and schools used as shelters for those who have become homeless. It is definitely not the right time for such grandiose philosophical questions. But what is the Palestinian to do when she or he lives such a crude political reality?

This article does not claim to be a reasonable political analysis of the "Gaza conflict" and "violent clashes" that erupted recently in the Gaza Strip. Nor does it claim to be an analysis that investigates the background and expected outcome of what many Palestinian activists consider the end of Oslo. It, therefore, should not fall into the mind-body bourgeois dichotomy. Emotions at this historical junction cannot be ignored.

* Originally published in a slightly different form in Haidar Eid, "The Rape of Gaza," Opinion, *Al-Jazeera*, July 31, 2014, aljazeera.com. Reprinted with permission from the publisher.

Consider this: While I was writing this article, a dozen Palestinian civilians were killed; more than thirteen hundred have been killed as Gaza massacre begins its twenty-fourth day; rights groups say 80 percent of the dead are civilians. And Israeli attacks seem to be on the rise. The (unpuzzling) question that Palestinians have been asking, and answering, is: How can a government that claims commitment to peace with its "Palestinian partner" order its soldiers to shoot and kill indiscriminately?

The importance of the image in Walter Benjamin's *The Work of Art in the Age of Mechanical Reproduction* lies in its ability to convey an instant message.[15] For many, the only source of information is what they see on their TV screens. The footage of headless toddlers, has, therefore, become the direct message that Palestinians want to use to convey: "This is our daily political reality. This is where we have reached twenty years after the signing of the Oslo Accords." So much for the peace process and the two-state solution!

Yet mainstream media has systematically sanitized the images that have been coming out of Gaza to present a more "acceptable" picture of violence.

To echo Edward Said and Noam Chomsky, how can the international—read Western—media be objective when they are controlled by five transnational corporations, all of which have intimate relationships with the US defence industry? Are the more than two hundred children killed in Gaza only "regrettable" collateral damage?

What about the twenty-eight families that were completely wiped out while having their breakfast? And the children in Shujayea who bled to death for hours while their parents watched because the Israeli soldiers refused to let an ambulance approach the area? And the entire Abu Jamei family being killed when their four-storey home was targeted by an Israeli fighter jet? How many more are "acceptable collateral damage" for the Western media? The Hamads in Beit Hanoun? The Hajjs in Khan Younis? The Syams in Rafah? The Zaanins? Kanan and Saji Al-Hallaque, massacred together with their father, pregnant mother, grandmother, and aunt while the family was breaking their fast at Iftar. And their grandfather, my colleague Professor Akram Hallaque, has to live now with the pain of losing his family—wife, daughter (my student), two grandchildren, and pregnant daughter-in-law. His son has been in intensive care for days now.

Who will bring justice to them? Who will be made to pay for the loss of these families? Negotiations brokered by Obama and Kerry on behalf of the Israelis? War criminal Tony Blair? Are they supposed to see a nonsovereign state of West Bank and Gaza as a "fair" deal for the lives of the dear ones they have lost?

Those who have been killed had lived such short lives, all of it in the Gaza Strip—a life lived and lost as refugees under brutal Israeli occupation. It's our fate: to die in the 2006 war, or if not, in the 2008–09 war. Or if you've survived, then another attempt in 2012, and if still living, then they'd finish you off in 2014, or next time in 2015, 2016, 2017, 2021, 2023!

But is this enough for them? No! Gaza is a challenge to the Israeli regime because here two-thirds of the population are refugees who are entitled to the right of return under UN Resolution 194. Could this be the real reason Israel is committing genocide on Gaza repeatedly? Kill the "brute" and live happily ever after?!

Gaza has become a permanent war zone; the biggest concentration camp on earth has become a burial site—a noisy graveyard. The Palestinian body has become the ultimate target of the Israeli bullet—the younger, the better! The Palestinian body has, in other words, become the site of (in)justice: eliminate the body and it will leave a vacuum that can be occupied—a land without people for people without land.

The Palestinian people have long realized that the so-called peace process does not challenge or change the long-held status quo, nor will it allow them to exercise their national and political rights.

Right or Left, the Israeli position is crystal clear: No return to the borders of June 4, 1967, no dismantling of Jewish settlements, no return of Palestinian refugees, no backing down on Jerusalem as the undivided eternal capital city of Israel, and no sovereign, independent Palestinian state with its own military on the western bank of the Jordan river.

The best that is on offer is a Palestinian Bantustan, a reservoir for the unwanted natives. And the people in Gaza don't even deserve that undignified solution: better to get rid of them all with a final solution via genocide with the support of the US president, European countries, the Arab League, and even some native Palestinians! Hearing these powerful instigators and supporters of the genocide bleating for a ceasefire twenty-four days after such a huge massacre adds insult to injury!

The Palestinians of Gaza get blamed for being shot and bombed because they did not run away; they get blamed for being in the same building that they have lived in all their short, brutal lives; they get blamed for not being able to run in fifty-seven seconds; they get blamed for letting their children play on the beach.

And they get blamed for refusing to let the colonizer, the occupier, the oppressor, the murderer, and its allies dispossess them and dishonour their dead with their false words, their biased media channels, their fake empathy, and their useless shuttle diplomacy that has no intention of giving Palestinians their rights under international law. Hence, the unprecedented brutality, the shelling with heavy artillery—what Joseph Conrad's Kurtz calls "The horror! The horror!"[16] The horror that embodies itself in the faces of those children who have lost their lives in Bibi's death chambers.

August 27, 2014

THE OTHERING OF GAZA

There is no such thing as a Palestinian.
—Golda Meir

The old will die and the young will forget.
—Ben Gurion

Israelis have many things to say about Palestinians, none of them humanizing or related to reality.* They continue to create their false narrative, making Orwellian words their allies. From 1948 to today, words have been a weapon as important as their army, their navy, and their air force.

Their words and their machinery of death have created a situation in Gaza today that defies description. The lack of water and electricity, the inability to find bodies under massive piles of rubble because bare hands can only do so much, the barbarism of targeting children. Words are so inadequate to express the anger and trauma, the resilience and the solidarity.

Where is one to begin and end if one wants to present a "neutral" analysis of the "dramatic" footage of the massive "surgical" explosions of the five multistorey residential apartment blocks (two as high as thirteen storeys) located in densely populated areas in Gaza City and Rafah.

Tellingly, a Western journalist interviewing me on these war crimes had this to say: "But Israel is saying that these apartment blocks were used as headquarters for Khamas [sic]?" To which I replied:" Israel could have said that these residential towers had the body of Hitler buried under them, and that they had nuclear war

* Originally published in a slightly different form in Haidar Eid, "Gaza, the Goy!" *Al-Jazeera,* August 27, 2014, aljazeera.com. Reprinted with permission from the publisher.

heads hidden there, and you would nevertheless, still ask the same question and expect me to respond to that 'neutral' question!"

It never occurred to this journalist to consider that this destruction of the homes of tens of families is unjustified irrespective of what was under the building. That there was anything whatsoever underneath has not been proven in any way whatsoever.

Take the footage of the children injured and bleeding to death in these attacks. In spite of Israel's attempts to convince us that militants were the target, and not these children, is this a rationale that we are supposed to accept when Israel bombs residential blocks housing families? And those same "militants" that are targeted today were perhaps the five-year-olds of 1967, or the children of the First Intifada in 1987, or maybe the children of the Second Intifada in 2000.

So it is Palestine's children that Israel is targeting because we are all Palestine's children, irrespective of how old we are. And the Israeli war machine has been targeting us for sixty-five long years with increasing brutality and viciousness with every minute that goes by and with each new technological discovery that enhances their ability to kill and maim with the gruesome sophistication of twenty-first century warfare.

If there were questions to be asked, it would be to question their need to make their presence felt by reducing homes, shopping malls, and markets to rubble with increasing regularity. It would be to question their indiscriminate killing of anyone in their path and crudely calling it "mowing the lawn." It would be to question the leaders of the world and the multilateral organizations that fail to act in spite of the loud voices of the people of the world demanding such action.

The war today is an echo of the war of 2012, and that is a reminder of the war of 2009, and before that the war of 2008, and still before the war of 1967, 1956, and 1948. The war of today, therefore, is an echo of the 1948 Nakba, and the 1967 Naksa, and Sabra and Shatila in 1983.

Those wars are in our genes and in our memories, whether we were there or not. They are part of our collective memory and our collective trauma, our collective and individual unconscious. We remember them from the stories we were told and we see them in our lives from 1948. Edward Said calls it "the Palestinian narrative" that should be registered. War after war, an unending Nakba. Our parents' experiences mix with our current reality. They could not protect us when we were children and now we cannot protect our children. We try, but they know as well as we do that this war, like the ones before, comes in wherever it wants to, and there are no places too sacred for it.

Shujayea: Massacre at Dawn

But we are not just cannon fodder for Israeli soldiers. We are not just victims trying to save our families. We have our memories of the olive trees we left behind, the warmth of the earth and the smell of the zaa'tar and *marameyya** on the hillside of the West Bank. We have the keys to our homes and the "knowledge" that this land is our land. We are here and we will not be ignored nor will we be exterminated. We are the rightful owners of this land, and we will pass on this heritage to the next generation.

The Israeli killing machine is frustrated by our refusal to die: to be ethnically cleansed like so many Native Americans and Aboriginal Australians. They vent their anger because we "force" them to kill us, because we "make" them look bad, because we subvert their victim narrative. The Israeli killing machine would not be able to do its job without the support of the United States and the emasculated United Nations.

So they gather together in the capitals of the world and pontificate in public and call for a ceasefire between the "two sides," unconditional, immediate. If there is something the oppressed Palestinian hates, other than Zionist racism and wrath, it is the complicity of Europe and the US, a complicity that considered Nelson Mandela the arch terrorist of the twentieth century!

But of course we know that this handwringing and pontification is meaningless because they have been doing this for decades: under British Mandate Palestine and with a succession of presidents and secretaries general. Loud noises, flurry of travel and

* Sage.

meetings, and no action: The failure to act is not accidental but deliberate, a ploy to divert public attention while still keeping all the power in the hands of apartheid Israel.

So far, just in this war, and to bring to an end the illegal, hermetic siege of Gaza, 2,142 killed, 490 of whom are children, 260 of whom are women, 101 of whom are elderly. More than 11,000 Palestinians have been injured, many with permanent disabilities and serious life-changing brain and other injuries. How many more wars and deaths and injuries and destroyed homes and apartment blocks will it take to end Israeli occupation, colonialism, and apartheid?

The prevailing feeling here in Gaza is that if the world does not intervene decisively, Israel is intent on slaughtering us all. And the technology and sophistication of modern warfare to do this is already in the hands one of the world's most powerful armies, so our fear that they will kill us all is not unfounded.

The support of civil society around the world has been a source of immense encouragement in these dark days and painful nights. The voices of those outside the centres of power have shown us loudly and clearly that they are walking this journey with us. The support of countries from the South speak of their experience of racism, colonialism, and dispossession. Our occupation is their history. Our struggle their shame. Governments of the world will not act until their citizens demand action from them, and our brothers and sisters around the world have made their demands known loudly and clearly. This kind of citizen activism has worked in other countries and it will work for us too.

The BDS movement is growing daily. Civil society has roared their rejection of apartheid Israel on the streets of world capitals. That roar must continue and move even deeper into churches, mosques, temples, unions, universities, and schools. It must be seen in supermarkets and in the boycott of companies that sell Israeli products. It must be heard ever louder in parliaments and sports fields, increasing the isolation of apartheid Israel. That roar must drown out the words and actions of apartheid Israel and allow Palestinians to breathe, to speak, to write, to live!

February 12, 2015

ON GAZA AND GLOBAL RAGE

On August 9, 2014, hundreds of thousands of people worldwide took to the streets in response to a call from Palestinian civil society in the occupied and besieged Gaza Strip, and the Boycott, Divestment, Sanctions National Committee (BNC), for a Day of Rage.*

This mobilization comes as grassroots pressure mounts on complicit Western governments to impose a military embargo on Israel. In its call for a Day of Rage, Palestinian civil society made it absolutely clear what they hoped to achieve:

> As we face the full might of Israel's military arsenal, funded and supplied by the United States and the European Union, we call on civil society and people of conscience throughout the world to pressure governments to sanction Israel and implement a comprehensive arms embargo immediately. Take to the streets . . . with a united demand for sanctions on Israel.

In response to an earlier call issued by the same civil society organizations in Gaza, and endorsed by the BNC, Spain announced a "provisional" suspension of military exports to Israel on July 31. On August 7, Evo Morales, president of Bolivia, became the first head of state to declare his support for BDS. These actions were a precursor to the global support for Gaza and Palestine shown on August 9.

The Israeli wrath inflicted on the Palestinians of Gaza, two-thirds of whom are refugees, entitled to the right of return, comes within an ideological context of tribal bigotry, racism, and exclusivism. In 2004, Israeli Professor Arnon Soffer, Head of the Israeli

* Originally published in a slightly different form in Haidar Eid, "On Gaza and Global Rage," Opinion, *Middle East Eye*, February 12, 2015, middleeasteye.net. Reprinted with permission from the publisher.

Occupation Force's National Defence College and adviser to Ariel Sharon, spelled out Israel's macabre expectation from the unilateral Israeli disengagement from Gaza (2005) in an interview with *Jerusalem Post*:

> When 1.5 million people live in a closed-off Gaza, it's going to be a human catastrophe. Those people will become even bigger animals than they are today . . . The pressure at the border will be awful. It's going to be a terrible war. So, if we want to remain alive, we will have to kill and kill and kill. All day, every day.. . If we don't kill, we will cease to exist . . . Unilateral separation doesn't guarantee "peace"—it guarantees a Zionist-Jewish state with an overwhelming majority of Jews.

Then, there is the view bluntly expressed in 2002 by Israel's then chief of staff, General Moshe Yaalon, which sums up the objective of the current blood bath: "The Palestinians must be made to understand in the deepest recesses of their consciousness that they are a defeated people."

The resemblance of Israel's campaign of tribal racist hate both to that of apartheid South Africa and to Hitler's murderous regime has recently been articulated by African National Congress (ANC) freedom fighter and former South African cabinet minister, Ronnie Kasrils, who is Jewish:

> Certainly we South Africans can identify the pathological cause, fuelling the hate, of Israel's political-military elite and public in general. Neither is this difficult for anyone acquainted with colonial history to understand the way in which deliberately cultivated race hate inculcates a justification for the most atrocious and inhumane actions against even defenceless civilians—women, children, the elderly amongst them. In fact was this not the pathological racist ideology that fuelled Hitler's war lust and implementation of the Holocaust?[17]

The Israeli establishment's stated goal of annihilating Palestinians to manage the "demographic threat" and to maintain "calm" by "mowing the lawn" (Israeli-speak for flattening Gaza every two years) is exactly why we in Palestine have concluded that the Palestinian struggle for self-determination must work to isolate apartheid Israel in the same way that apartheid South Africa was isolated through a campaign of BDS.

Today, there is a growing mass-based struggle inside Palestine, as well as other forms of struggle, exactly as there was inside apartheid South Africa. An intensified international solidarity movement with a common agenda can make the struggle for Palestine resonate in every country in the world, thus closing off the world to Israelis until they open the world to Palestinians.

It is evident today that the Palestinian BDS campaign, modelled on the South African anti-apartheid global campaign, is gaining momentum as a democratic movement based on the struggle for human rights and implementation of international law. This is the antithesis of what Zionism, Israel's hegemonic ideology, is all about: religious, ethnic, and racial; our struggle, like that of the Black natives of South Africa and African Americans of the America South, is inclusive and universalistic: one that guarantees the rehumanization of our people in the face of a genocidal machine run by what Moshe Dayan would have called "a mad dog."[18]

This is exactly what Steve Biko, a hero of the South African anti-apartheid struggle—who paid with his life for the freedom of all South Africans—meant when he said:

> Not only have the whites been guilty of being on the offensive, but by some skilful manoeuvres, they have managed to control the responses of the Blacks to the provocation. Not only have they kicked the Black, but they have also told him how to react to the kick. For a long time the Black has been listening with patience to the advice he has been receiving on how best to respond to the kick. With painful slowness he is now beginning to show signs that it is his right and duty to respond to the kick in the way he sees fit.[19]

And we, Palestinians, have decided to respond to the Zionist kick in the way we see fit! And for that, we need the support of the conscientious world, as opposed to the complicit, official world whose leaders have decided to blame the victim instead. Now is the time to help us kick racism and genocidal bigotry by boycotting the apartheid Israeli state, by divesting and imposing sanctions against it. This is the only way to ensure peace with justice in the Middle East.

The global masses that demonstrated their support for Palestinian rights on the Day of Rage remind us of the demonstrations in the 1980s against apartheid South Africa. These global protests since 2009 have shown us in Palestine that this is our "South Africa moment." Just as the South African internal mass-based anti-apartheid struggle and the international anti-apartheid boycott and solidarity movement brought an end to the apartheid regime, Palestinians, with the support of people of conscience worldwide, will bring an end to Israel's multitiered system of oppression.

Governments across the world must be forced to act in accordance with the will of their people and hold Israel accountable for war crimes and impose sanctions and an arms embargo. People of conscience globally have spoken and their voices have reached us here in Gaza. We know that their voices have been heard in the capitals of the world and that their voices signal an end to Israeli apartheid. The clock is ticking.

Hence the importance of the Gaza Day of Rage!

April 2, 2015

ISRAEL

Mainstream Western Media's Blind Spot

The history of Palestinian exile and Diaspora has been overshadowed and almost silenced by the story of other exiles, most prominently that of European Jews during Hitler's "final solution."* This genocide of Jewish people, which has come to be called the Holocaust, has subsequently received fifty years of attention in films, books, and conferences and this memory has been institutionalized in Holocaust museums in many countries. Only recently has attention begun to be paid to the decades-long Palestinian experience of dispossession, massacres, and human suffering.

This apartheid-like nightmare that Palestinians endure is the planned and deliberate impact of the hundreds of draconian Israeli laws and actions aimed at humiliating the unarmed and defenceless Palestinian people. The ultimate objective of this strategy is to undermine and silence any possibility of establishing a sovereign, independent Palestinian state.

Western mainstream media outlets seem to intentionally disregard many facts when reporting on Palestine. These outlets claim to be "objective," but a cursory review of their reporting shows that the levels of blindness to Palestinian realities can only be the result of the biased ideology of the media outlet itself. This reporting tends to deliberately ignore the following:

The West Bank and Gaza Strip, including East Jerusalem, are still occupied territories. This is a descriptive phrase that has disappeared from the political lexicon describing the conflict, even though it refers to the official position of the vast majority of countries in the world.

* Originally published in a slightly different form in Haidar Eid, "Israel: Mainstream Western Media's Blind Spot," Opinion, *Middle East Eye*, April 2, 2015, middleeasteye.net. Reprinted with permission from the publisher.

Military occupation, by definition, involves various types of violence: it violates rights and due process and uses direct force as its main instrument of rule. Israel is the last occupying power in the world, an anachronism in the twenty-first century. Clause 50 of the 1907 Hague Convention states unequivocally the international community's rejection of collective punishment; this was reiterated by the Fourth Geneva Convention in the Clause 33 of 1949. Resistance to occupation is guaranteed under international law, and the occupation is the root cause of violence and terrorism.

The Palestinian Authority (PA) controls an area that comprises less than 20 percent of the total area of the West Bank and Gaza Strip. The PA has administrative control over the population but has no sovereignty over land or borders. Palestine does not exist as a state. Palestinians do not have an army. Israel is a state. Israelis do have the strongest army in the Middle East and the fourth strongest in the world. Israel, the occupying force, is also a nuclear power.

The resistance, be it the BDS movement or popular uprisings, is a response to Israeli occupation, colonization, and apartheid. Tens of thousands of Palestinian lives have been lost during the almost sixty-seven-year struggle to regain Palestinian independence, with the majority of these being ordinary Palestinians, or civilians, including hundreds of children younger than sixteen.

Israel is not the state of its citizens but rather "the state of the Jews." What happens to the Palestinians who did not leave during the 1947–1948 pogroms but instead became citizens of the state formed in 1948? They exist as third-class citizens in the Israel of today, but no Western media outlet highlights this lack of equality, choosing instead to single out Israel as the only "democracy in the Middle East."

The United States of America has not called on Israel to have a constitution that is as inclusive as its own—which means creating a state for all of the citizens of Israel irrespective of religion, race, or ethnicity. It has rather allowed and supported Israel to create and maintain a state for Jews only, and continues to justify this at every opportunity that it gets. Where is the Western media's focus on the anomaly of Western governments calling Israel a democracy when it is in fact a theocracy?

There are repeated claims that Palestinians rejected great deals at Camp David and with the Oslo Accords. However, the current political stalemate began when one-third of the Palestinian people, namely the residents of the Gaza Strip and the West Bank, rejected the Oslo Accords and the two-state solution in legislative council elections in 2006. The "generous offer" given to them by the "dovish" Zionist "Left" in these accords was going to be a nonsovereign, truncated "state" in return for a final termination of all rights and claims to historical Palestine, including the right of return of Palestinian refugees. In any event, even if Palestinians had accepted the deal, it is not clear that it could have been accepted and imposed within Israel.

The Israeli-Palestinian "conflict" is not intractable and "too complex to understand." It will be solved if Israel withdraws to the 1967 borders in accordance with the "land for peace" formula embodied in relevant UN resolutions, implements UN Resolution 194, and ends its discriminatory policies against its Palestinian citizens. This is still the official position of the majority of mainly developing and nonaligned countries in the world. The reason for the current uprisings and tension in the Arab world is Israeli occupation, colonization, and apartheid.

The plight of the six thousand Palestinian political prisoners has attracted little attention outside Israel, even though there have been warnings from human rights groups about the dire conditions they endure. Some of these prisoners are on an open-ended hunger strike, to expose the systematic abuse and torture they experience in Israeli prisons.*

None of these facts are part of the mainstream Western media reports because for them, Palestinian lives simply do not count. They are not worth a word of empathy from the first-ever elected African American president of the US, nor from CNN, the *New York Times*, or the BBC. Their lack of reporting on these facts enables Israel to hide behind the facade of the "peace process" and the title of "the only democracy in the Middle East."

* The number has risen to 10,200 since the October 7, 2023.

Aside from this failure in mainstream Western media reporting, there are two main reasons for Israel's decades-long failure to comply with international law. First, public opinion in Israel has been drifting to the right for the past three decades and, as a result, the "Eretz Israel"* ideology has become increasingly influential in Israeli politics. The fact that Israel has been able to occupy Palestinian land with impunity for forty-seven years has contributed to this colonizing mindset.

Second, the Oslo process was designed to be a "negotiated process." An important fact is masked by this empty phrase. It is this: negotiations will take place under a balance of power wholly in Israel's favour, with US support at every turn, while Israeli settlements increase and Israel's colonial drive continues unabated. If the "process" stalls or fails, there is a built-in villain to attribute blame to.

While public attention focused on other wars in the Middle East over the last thirty years, successive Israeli governments have continued to create new Jewish colonies in the Occupied Territories, by confiscating land, assassinating leaders of the Palestinian resistance, and withdrawing residence permits from Palestinians born in "strategic areas"—including Jerusalem.

They have also closed Palestinian schools, tortured Palestinian political prisoners, destroyed orchards and greenhouses, and steadily decreased the ability of Palestinians to support themselves and their families while increasing their dependence on Israeli-grown products. Since 1948, hundreds of thousands of Palestinian houses have been destroyed, with many people made homeless twice, thrice, or even four times in their lives.

After enduring this ongoing Nakba since 1948, and since the brutal Israeli invasions of the Gaza Strip in 2009, 2012, and 2014 were documented by citizen journalists in Palestine and broadcast worldwide, the mainstream Western media bias can no longer be hidden from view.

* Eretz Israel is a Zionist philosophical and theological concept that refers to Israel as the Holy Land, the land God promised to the Jewish people. This philosophical concept has become a political doctrine that claims Jewish right to the land and denies Palestinian's rights.

It is obvious to informed readers and viewers that the much-vaunted objectivity and reporting of only the facts of both sides of the story has been long thrown aside when it comes to the question of Palestine. What we have instead is embedded journalists who cover the story only to misrepresent the facts to support their governments' continued enabling of Israeli occupation, colonization, and apartheid.

April 6, 2016

PALESTINIAN REFLECTIONS ON ISRAEL'S HYSTERICAL ATTACK ON BDS

In their extremist incitement against the BDS movement, Israeli leaders, from right to extreme-right, made it absolutely clear that they were serious about seeing the end of the movement before it achieves its objectives, namely freedom, justice, and equality.* They have labelled the BDS movement a "strategic threat" to Israel's system of occupation, colonization, and apartheid, adopted and enforced by the ruling Zionist establishment. At the Yediot Ahronot "Stop BDS" Conference, minister after minister, leader after leader, used inflammatory rhetoric that must be very familiar to anti-South African apartheid movement activists, most of whom must have felt a sense of déjà vu listening to the tirade.

Interior Minister Aryeh Deri called for the expulsion of BDS leaders because "you cannot turn the other cheek to those who beat us."

The most serious threat, however, came from the minister of intelligence, Israel Katz, who used intentionally ambiguous language to send a message of terror to Palestinian and international BDS activists: "You had better stop BDS, or we will resort to 'civic assassination!'" He went to on to explain what he meant by that:

> [It] is to expose the actors, the people, the system, the mechanisms and their connections to the organizations that have already crossed the threshold of military and terrorist activity. And definitely, through this exposure, to know how to act against them, how to isolate them, also to transfer information

* Originally published in a slightly different form in Haidar Eid, "Palestinian Reflections on Israel's Hysterical Attack on BDS," *Mondoweiss*, April 6, 2016, mondoweiss.net. Reprinted with permission from the publisher.

> to intelligence agents around the world, and other agents. We have to understand that there is a battle here. It is wrapped in many covers.

This is not news anymore! But what does it mean to those of us, BDS activists, based in Palestine?

I, myself, live in besieged Gaza. I have witnessed three huge massacres committed by apartheid Israel, almost lost my life more than once, and lost very close comrades, colleagues, relatives, and students. I have lived through an indescribable, ongoing trauma and seen horror beyond words. I have been prevented from attending my parents' funerals, deprived of seeing my sister and nephews who live in Bethlehem, a one-hour drive away, for more than sixteen years, and have been without a consistent source of electricity and clean water since 2006. I have seen the Baker children being slaughtered in broad daylight on a Gaza beach, read with agony the names of sixty-six families that were totally wiped out by Israeli weapons and deleted from the civic registry. I had to consciously fight against the possibility of becoming just a number in a news report on CNN, BBC, and Sky News. Twenty-two hundred people, including 551 children, were not that lucky in 2014! Nor were 1200, including 443 children, in 2006, or 2009, or 2012! The Israeli war machine and the international conspiracy of silence took their lives.

And now I am being told that by calling nonviolently for Israeli accountability, which is what BDS does, and in spite of the failure of the so-called international community to hold apartheid Israel accountable for war crimes and crimes against humanity, my colleagues and I would be targeted for "civic assassination" unless we are quiet and become "good, native boys and girls"—Uncle Tom of the state of Israel.

So, what have we done to drive Israel's leaders, right and extreme-right, to the brink of madness? After all that we have gone through from 1948 until today, does apartheid Israel really think that we would budge? Did the icons of the anti-apartheid anti-colonial movements show any sign of weakness in the face of similar threats? Did the millions of South Africans, African Americans, and Indians stop their fight against apartheid, inequality, and colonialism in the face of such threats? They did not, and the names of leaders such as Mahatma Gandhi, Nelson Mandela, Steve Biko, Martin Luther King, Rosa Parks are but a few whose names live on today. Gandhi told us, "First they ignore you, then they laugh at you, then they fight you, then you win." And judging by the achievements of the BDS movement over the last ten years, we can say that we are winning. Mandela reminded us all that "South Africa's freedom is incomplete without the freedom of the Palestinians." He would be arrested, if not assassinated, for saying something like this in Israel today!

Steve Biko, founder of the Black Consciousness Movement, cannot escape my mind. His racist murderers are now in the dustbin of history; so are Ariel Sharon, Menachem Begin, Yitzhak Shamir, even Yitzhak Rabin, Moshe Dayan, and soon all those Israeli ministers and opposition leaders who consider the call for freedom and equality an "existential threat!"

The real tragedy of post-Oslo Palestine is not that the majority of Palestinians had no say in whether or not they wanted this new "administrative autonomy"; rather, it is that we have never been given the tools to negotiate our new reality. Isn't it glaringly obvious by now that apartheid Israel signed the Oslo Accords and gave us "limited autonomy" only because this costs Tel Aviv less?!

Herein comes the importance of our BDS movement, as it represents the expression of our determination to develop our own voice, a new vision of freedom from occupation, and our desire to accomplish justice and equality. BDS, in different words, is driven by our own desire to decolonize and de-Osloize our minds in our fight to forge an emancipatory Palestinian subject of liberation away from the hallucinatory facade of "independence."

To claim that the fight for equality and justice is antisemitic is not unlike saying that Mandela was racist and Gandhi was violent. Our choices, as BDS activist, are limited: we either follow in the footsteps of Biko, Mandela, Gandhi, Parks, King, or we switch sides and take the infamous Bantustan leaders like the Mangopes and Buthelezis of this world as our role models.

We've taken the first option because that is the only choice that will lead us to a free Palestine, with peace and justice for all its inhabitants.

June 16, 2017

ONE QUESTION LEFT IN GAZA

Death by Massacre or Lack of Electricity?

Like everywhere else in the world, electricity in Gaza gives us access to clean water and medical care.* With it, we can refrigerate our food in the hot summer and find warmth in the cold winter—and connect with the outside world and one another.

It may sound very benign—electricity has been cut to Gaza—but it is a death sentence for the almost two million Gazans like me living in the Israeli-imposed blockaded Strip.

In fact, cutting electricity to Gaza is a de facto declaration of war against the civilian population and an illegal form of collective punishment.

For those who are not familiar, the debate among Gazans nowadays is whether a direct military assault—that is the use of bombs and guns carried out by apartheid Israel—is a better way to die than through an incremental genocide, the intensifying blockade that has been imposed on our tiny Strip for ten years.

Just think about that: Are there citizens in any other country in the world who debate what the better way is for them to die?

Gideon Levy, the courageous Israeli journalist, has an answer: "What's at stake now is the danger of another massacre in the Gaza Strip. Controlled, measured, not too massive, but nonetheless a massacre. When Israeli officers, politicians and commentators talk about 'the next round,' they're talking about the next massacre."

The Palestinian Authority's Means and Ends

Apartheid Israel has maintained a deadly medieval blockade on Gaza since 2007, when the Islamic Resistance Movement, Hamas,

* Originally published in a slightly different form in Haidar Eid, "One Question Left in Gaza: Death by Massacre or Lack of Electricity?" *Middle East Eye*, June 16, 2017, middleeasteye.net. Reprinted with permission from the publisher.

seized control of the tiny Strip after legitimately winning the 2006 Legislative Council elections.

This blockade was imposed because the democratic choice of the Palestinians was rejected outright by almost all major powers in the region, including the Fatah-led PA.

The siege has recently become even worse because in April, Mahmoud Abbas, the president of the PA, asked Israel to cut the electricity supply to the Gaza Strip to exert pressure on Hamas.

This followed his decision, also in April, to reduce the salaries of Gaza-based civil servants by 30 percent. It should be obvious to any reader that the occupants of Gaza are not just the leaders of Hamas but ordinary Palestinians too. We are the people who are enduring these salary and electricity cuts.

Even after a decade-long blockade, the situation here in Gaza is the worst it's ever been following these latest changes. Hospitals, including Al-Shifa in Gaza City, have stopped doing operations, even in urgent cases.

As a result of the electricity cuts, 90 percent of the water supply is now undrinkable, increasing the risk of disease spread by dirty water.

The PA has reduced its monthly payments for electricity by 30 percent. And so Israel has allowed only 40 watts of power to be provided to the Strip in the full knowledge that 400 watts are needed for Gaza to meet the bare minimum survival needs.

Repeat Warnings

It's not like the world hasn't been warned—repeatedly.

In mid-May, the International Committee of the Red Cross (ICRC) warned of the imminent collapse of the Gaza Strip, saying, in a grim statement, "The scarcity of energy and the severe shortage of fuel in Gaza have damaged all aspects of life in the Strip." The statement warned of a "looming crisis" in the public health and environment sectors as a result of the lack of energy.

And back in September 2015, the UN warned that Gaza could be "uninhabitable" by 2020. At the time, the report made it clear that Gaza's GDP had dropped by 15 percent in 2014 and unemployment had reached a record high of 44 percent, with 72 percent of households being food insecure. The report concluded that Gaza's de-development had been accelerated by the Israeli assault on Gaza in 2014.

This month, the UN acknowledged that without immediate action, the electricity crisis will bring about the "collapse of vital life-saving, health, water, sanitation and municipal services." But, strangely, the UN does not seem to have a grip on international law; the UN apportions blame for this crisis on the occupied Palestinians, not the Israeli occupier.

On the other hand, Richard Falk, the previous UN special rapporteur on the situation of human rights in the Palestinian territories called a spade a spade, saying that he considered the siege on Gaza a "flagrant and massive violation of international humanitarian law" and a "crime against humanity." Israeli writer Ilan Pappé also rightly calls it an "incremental genocide."[20]

What Has Become Routine

The terror of it is that Gazans die every day, but death from illness as a result of dirty water or the lack of a lifesaving operation, starvation due to the crops that fail to grow without sufficient irrigation, or babies dying because they cannot be kept warm in their first few days of life, these ways of dying do not make the news headlines.

Gazan deaths do not make the news headlines because they have been a daily routine for a decade. Only Israel benefits from this silence, and only Gazans pay the price for this silence.

Gideon Levy again: "To the Israelis, Gaza was and is a nest of terrorists . . . all its residents are murderous. They're building terror tunnels instead of inaugurating high-tech plants. No, really, how come Hamas hasn't developed Gaza? How dare they? How have they not set up an industry under siege, agriculture in prison, and high-tech in a cage?"

It needs to be understood by the outside world that there is not much that we in Gaza can do against this medieval blockage except call on our supporters to intensify their call for boycott, divestment, and sanctions against Israel. Every single victory of the BDS movement supports Gaza's survival.

The international community has utterly failed us. *Period.*

Words and empty rhetoric do not keep a Palestinian child crying out for milk alive, nor does it provide a terminally ill person with treatment.

We have just one window of hope, the same window that Black South Africans saw before us—a sustained campaign of boycott, divestment, and sanctions against apartheid Israel until it complies with international law.

July 14, 2017

GAZA AND THE FAILURE OF THE NATIONAL PROJECT

In order to understand the draconian measures taken by the Fatah-led PA against the Gaza Strip, which has already been enduring a suffocating, decade-long Israeli siege, one has to scrutinize the Fatah movement's diminished ideological and national agenda.*

There is already a humanitarian crisis in Gaza, documented by international, local, and Israeli human rights organizations. To add insult to injury, Israel has imposed severe restrictions on the import of construction materials needed for rebuilding the thousands of homes and institutions destroyed during the 2014 Israeli onslaught.

Palestinians of Gaza do understand that the Israeli siege is rooted in the history of Zionist settler colonialism, where the native is completely dehumanized and her death is not counted.

The Gaza Strip is itself a large refugee camp—70 percent of its two million residents are refugees—a reminder of the original sin committed in 1948, when Zionist militias and later the Israeli army expelled more than 750,000 Palestinians from their original homes.

Israel is motivated to finish the job, to make sure that the unwanted surplus population is kept in a large prison, but without naming it as such.

And at the same time, those ungrateful "Arabs" of Gaza must understand that the siege is their fate since it is supported by a complicit international community, Arab regimes, and—most importantly—some of their own leaders. Hence comes the idea that Gaza is a place of infinite darkness, figuratively and literally.

* Originally published in a slightly different form in Haidar Eid, "Gaza and the Failure of the National Project," *Electronic Intifada*, July 14, 2017, electronicintifada.net. Reprinted with permission from the publisher.

Immoral Decision

This unbearable humanitarian situation in Gaza is further compounded by the PA's decision in April to suspend payments to Israel for electricity for Gaza, and its decision to reinstate taxes on fuel destined for Gaza.

This ultimately caused a shutdown of Gaza's only power plant, which was already operating at reduced capacity due to damage sustained in repeated Israeli bombardments over the years, reducing electricity available to the Gaza Strip to the lowest levels ever.

Going even further, the PA has reduced funding to Gaza's hospitals and clinics as well as put into effect drastic pay cuts to public sector employees whose salaries have provided a vital stream of revenue in the besieged coastal Strip. For example, the salaries of Al-Aqsa University employees have been slashed by 80–90 percent for the fourth month in a row.

The latest immoral decision taken by the PA was to force six thousand Gaza civil servants, most of whom work in education and health, into early retirement.

All of these deadly measures have been taken in a bid to pressure Hamas, the de facto ruling party in Gaza,* into relinquishing its control and "reconciling" with the PA.

Some Fatah apologists have gone even further and claimed that all of these measures have been taken in defence of the "national project," which has supposedly been under tremendous threat by Hamas.

They fail to explain, however, how an academic's salary ended up being a "threat" to the national project.

Fatah's Self-Pitying Analysis

In order to understand the PA's measures against Gaza, one has to examine the weaknesses of Fatah—whose name is a reverse acronym for "Palestinian National Liberation Movement"—and its failure to achieve any of its declared goals, including its inability

* Hamas has been in control of the Gaza Strip since it won the Legislative Council elections in 2006. Those results were not accepted by the PA, which tried, with the support of the American administration, to topple the Hamas government in July 2007.

to accept its own defeat in the 2006 democratic elections for the Palestinian Legislative Council.

I would also argue that the latest PA strangulation of Gaza reflects not only the demise of Fatah—the faction that dominated the PLO for decades—but the demise of contemporary Palestinian nationalism in general.

Fatah started as a national liberation movement aiming to "liberate Palestine from the Jordan River to the Mediterranean Sea, through the barrel of the gun," but it has moved into the post-colonial condition without achieving a single gain in democracy, justice, or liberation for the Palestinian people.

It transformed into a Bantustan organization bearing the trappings of a nonexistent "state."

Through a mechanical and self-pitying analysis of the outcome of the 2006 elections and subsequent events in the Gaza Strip, Fatah has made its position clear: the dire humanitarian and political situation in the Gaza Strip has been caused by Hamas. And since most Gazans voted for Hamas, they have to pay this heavy price.

Fatah was the driving political force behind the Oslo Accords that the PLO signed with Israel in 1993, which have been associated with corruption and the selling-out of principles of self-determination as defined by international law, and of liberation.

Loss of Faith

As a right-wing party, Fatah has been unable to understand the enormous changes and the paradigm shift in politics in the Gaza Strip as a result of the three massacres Israel carried out between 2008 and 2014. These include a loss of faith in the ability of the current leadership to come up with any solution that guarantees justice, the dwindling support for the two-state solution, and the rise of the BDS movement. So Fatah leaders continue to reiterate the long-held misbelief that the Oslo Accords are the only political route to a Palestinian state.

This remains a stark indication of their loss of faith in the power of the Palestinian people to reclaim their land and rights. Their approach is a repudiation of the undeniable, unprecedented steadfastness shown by the people of Gaza, the growing forms of popular resistance in the West Bank, and the success of the global BDS movement.

Interestingly, the worst and most inaccurate comment made by Oslo supporters currently is that Oslo has nothing do with the situation and events in the Gaza Strip these days.

On the other hand, one wonders whether the de facto government in Gaza seriously believes that its new alliance of convenience with its political nemesis, former Fatah strongman Muhammad Dahlan, can provide a solution to Gaza's unending politically created challenges.

Dahlan was a mortal enemy of Hamas but fell out with Fatah boss and PA leader Mahmoud Abbas, meaning that Dahlan and Hamas are now making common cause.

Through the alliance with Dahlan, who is backed by the United Arab Emirates and close to the Egyptian regime, Hamas was able to secure a few days supply of fuel for Gaza's power plant.

But allowing a few litres of fuel through the Rafah crossing is pressure valve politics, nothing more.

Window of Hope

In an article for *Al-Shabaka*, I argued that Palestinians must consider "dis-participation" in the current political system, which has become illegitimate and ineffective.

The Gaza blockade comes in the context of Israel's intrinsic genocidal tendency as a settler-colonial project that is characterized by a multitiered system of oppression.

In order to address the "Gaza crisis," Israel, like apartheid South Africa before it, has to pay a heavy price.

This is what the BDS movement is doing. It is the only window of hope that we Gazans think will make an impact.

October 20, 2017

PESSOPTIMISTIC REFLECTIONS FROM BESIEGED GAZA

One cannot understand the deadly, medieval siege imposed on Gaza apart from Israel's settler colonialism in Palestine.* The horror inflicted on Gaza is, in fact, rooted in the political fragmentation caused by apartheid Israel, reinforced by the Oslo authority, and sparked by factional struggles over access to power in a Bantustan turned into a concentration camp.†

The rationale behind this genocidal blockade imposed by apartheid Israel, and supported by a complicit Middle East Quartet, is that we, two million Gazans, are expected to recognize Israel's right to exist on our ethnically cleansed villages from where we were expelled in 1948 and renounce our resistance as a form of violence. This is how this Crime of Collective Punishment is justified! The international community is basically telling us that we must collaborate with the occupiers in order to be accepted, that we must normalize apartheid and settler colonialism. If we don't do that, we are doomed then and must pay a heavy price with the lives of our children.

The question then is whether the indigenous population of South Africa were asked to recognize apartheid's right to exist. Or, to put it bluntly, whether Jewish victims of Nazism were expected to collaborate with the Nazi monster in order to be accepted as humans?!

The extent to which Zionists hate the people of Gaza is materialized in Israel's attempt to literally drown Gaza in shit. Did the

* Originally published in a slightly different form in Haidar Eid, "Pessoptimistic Reflections from Besieged Gaza," *Mondoweiss*, October 20, 2017, mondoweiss.net. Reprinted with permission from the publisher.

† The word "Pessoptimistic" is taken from Emile Habibi's masterpiece *The Secret Life of Saeed: The Pessoptimist* (Readers International, 1989). It is the result of merging the words pessimist (al-mutasha'em) and optimist (al-mutafa'el).

white supremacists of South Africa, or the Nazis of the Third Reich for that matter, or the KKK in the American South, ever think of constructing a sewage damn that cracked and spilled its contents on their victims?!

We've ultimately been reduced to a vegetative existence in a concentration camp, the largest open-air prison on earth.

But unlike the victims of Nazism, we keep reminding ourselves to be careful enough and not fall into the trap of believing that our cause is exceptional, albeit extreme.

I belong to a generation that did not witness the Nakba, a generation that was thought to be resigned to fifty years of military occupation and sixty-nine years of dispossession and apartheid. But we've decided to rise up and resist. Hence our call for BDS, inspired by the anti-apartheid movement and other struggles against settler colonialism.

The way I look at it is that by allowing Israel to impose this unprecedented blockade on two million civilians and launch three massive wars on them in 2008, 2012, and 2014, resulting in the deaths of four thousand and the maiming of tens of thousands of them, in addition to the destruction of the infrastructure, the post-WWII international community has failed to uphold principles of justice and peace. It is therefore incumbent on civil society to take the lead. Hence the hope created among Palestinians by the huge successes achieved by the BDS movement. It is, as I keep repeating, the only window of hope we victims of occupation, apartheid, and settler colonialism have in the era of Donald Trump and Benjamin Netanyahu.

Gaza 2018

LAND DAY MASSACRE

2018

GAZA IN A WORLD WITHOUT WALLS

What does a world without borders mean to a Palestinian living in the besieged Gaza Strip?* Or, put differently, what needs to be done in order to remove all the walls, physical and immaterial, surrounding the tiny coastal Strip, which is suffering under a multitiered system of oppression? In this essay, I will address the issue from a personal point of view and then move towards addressing the more pressing question of what is to be done.

I received my doctorate degree from the University of Johannesburg, which I joined in 1997, three years after the collapse of the walls imposed by the apartheid system, only to return to Palestine three years later to be confined within the walls of what has become the largest open-air prison on earth. In 2006, the US and Israel "allowed" Palestinians in the West Bank and Gaza to vote for their representatives in the Palestinian Legislative Council, the legislative body created in anticipation of an ever more elusive Palestinian state. The hope was that Palestinians would vote for a pro-American political force; such a hope was misplaced. Instead, an anti-American political power that opposed the futile negotiations process that had begun with the Oslo Agreements in 1993 won the 2005 elections. That was the beginning of the ongoing deadly blockade imposed on Gaza, home to two million people—two-thirds of whom are refugees—crowded into 360 square kilometres, making it the most densely populated area on earth.

Confinement did not begin with the current siege, but with the Oslo Accords. I will illustrate this experience with a personal story. In the year 2000, after finishing my degree in South Africa, I decided to return to start a teaching career at Al-Najah University

* Originally published in a slightly different form in Haidar Eid, "Gaza in a World Without Walls," in *Build Resistance Not Walls: A Reader for a World Without Walls, eds., The Palestinian Grassroots Anti-Apartheid Wall Campaign* (Stop the Wall), StopTheWall.org, November 9, 2019, stopthewall.org. Reprinted with permission from the publisher.

in Nablus in the West Bank. That was before the eruption of the Al-Aqsa Intifada, when there was "peace" and some people could use the so-called Safe Passage (controlled by Israel) between Gaza and the West Bank. I applied for the necessary permit and handed in the required documents from Al-Najah. One week later, I was told that my application was rejected—no reason was given. So, I tried another route. I went to Eretz checkpoint to apply for a magnetic card; a computer card that gives Israeli military access to all files the Shin Bet, the Israeli secret services, keep about the person. I had to stand and wait in a queue from six in the morning, hoping to be interviewed by an officer to find out as to why my "safe corridor" application was turned down. They kept me waiting until five in the evening and then asked me to leave. I have not been able to visit the West Bank since the First Intifada began in 1987. The Oslo Accords, in fact, initiated the siege.

Today, restrictions are much tighter. In 2005, Israel turned the Gaza Strip into the largest open-air prison with the largest population of inmates in the world. It cynically called this process a "withdrawal" of its illegal settlers who had, until then, colonized the area. The international conspiracy of silence towards the genocidal war taking place against the two million civilians in Gaza is effective complicity in these war crimes. The Gaza Strip is not only hermetically sealed by a wall but also with every conceivable tool of repression, including electric fences and watch towers manned by trigger-happy soldiers who shoot first and ask questions later. The thousands of Israeli soldiers surrounding Gaza shoot to kill any Palestinian trying to escape into Israel, usually in search of work, and sometimes simply food.

Let Me Elaborate

Last May, the ICRC warned of the imminent collapse of the Gaza Strip, saying, in a grim statement, "The scarcity of energy and the severe shortage of fuel in Gaza have damaged all aspects of life in the Strip" and warning of a "looming crisis" in the public health and environmental sectors due to lack of energy.

This was not the first of such warnings. In September 2015, the UN warned that Gaza could be "uninhabitable" by 2020. The report made it clear that Gaza's GDP had dropped by 15 percent in 2014, and unemployment had reached a record high of 44 percent, with 72 percent of households classified as food insecure. The report concluded that Gaza's "de-development" had been accelerated by the Israeli assault in 2014.

This situation is not an accident. Some years earlier, the Israeli media had revealed that the Israeli army had calculated the exact number of calories Gaza's residents would need to consume to only just survive and avoid malnutrition. And even years before that, Dov Weissglass, who served as adviser to the Israeli prime minister, summed up Israeli policy towards the most densely populated area on earth: "The idea is to put the Palestinians on a diet, but not to make them die of hunger."[21]

As a result of Israel's blockade on most imports and exports and other policies designed to punish us, about 70 percent of Gaza's workforce is now unemployed or without salary, according to the UN, and about 80 percent of its residents live in grinding poverty. About 1.2 million are now dependent for their day-to-day survival on food handouts from the UN or international agencies. An increasing number of Palestinian families in Gaza are unable to offer their children more than one meagre meal a day, often little more than rice and boiled lentils. Fresh fruit and vegetables are beyond the reach of many families. Meat and chicken are impossibly expensive. Gaza faces the rich waters of the Mediterranean, but fish are unavailable in its markets because the Israeli navy has curtailed the movements of Gaza's fishermen.

Gaza is not only short of raw textiles and other key goods but also paper, ink, and vital school supplies. One-third of Gaza's children started the school year missing necessary textbooks. Our university students come to lectures hungry and unable to concentrate. Of course, cutting us off from the world silences our voice, taking away any academic freedom Palestinians need to represent themselves. Having to think about basic needs on a daily basis makes it impossible to deal with other social and academic issues that are urgent in the society, setting the people of Gaza back intellectually and socially, to say nothing of the trauma inflicted by the violence of the siege.

It is a violation of international law to collectively punish more than a million people without even bothering to accuse them of a crime. But Israel has shrugged off the law, has ignored the repeated demands of the UN Security Council. It has also dismissed the International Court of Justice in The Hague.

Decades of demonizing Palestinians, in general, and Gazans, in particular, have led to their dehumanization and to the proliferation of stereotypes and sweeping generalizations about them that culminate in statements such as the assertion by Israel's former defence minister that "there are no innocents in Gaza."[22] The decades-long slow genocide inflicted on them and their incremental death, therefore, is not registered by the world's conscience. We fully understand that the deliberate withholding of food or the means to grow food or the access to food is yet another strategy of Israel's occupation, colonization, and apartheid in Palestine and, therefore, should be viewed as intentionally genocidal.

What Is to Be Done?

What exactly are Gazans, in particular, and Palestinians in general, demanding from the international community? As we embark on our long walk to freedom, we have come to the conclusion that we can no longer rely on governments. Only civil society is able to mobilize to demand the implementation of international law and put an end to Israel's impunity.

Our inspiration is the South African anti-apartheid movement. The intervention of civil society was effective in the late 1990s against the apartheid regime of white South Africa, and it can do the same thing in support of a just peace in Palestine.

Nothing will force Israel to abide by international law except people of conscience and international civil society. Without the intervention of the international community, which was effective against apartheid in South Africa, Israel will continue its war crimes and crimes against humanity. And that is exactly what happened in 2009, 2012, and 2014, when it launched massive attacks, killing thousands of civilians and injuring more, many of them women and children.

We must formulate the kind of response that could actually defeat the multitiered system of Zionist oppression, which includes occupation, ethnic cleansing, and apartheid. The moment the entire international community, that is civil society and governments, decides to act the same way it did against the apartheid system of white South Africa, Israel would have to bow to the voice of reason represented by the call for boycotts, divestment, and sanctions, which was issued in 2005 by more than 170 civil society organizations and endorsed by almost all Palestinian political and social forces inside our homeland and in the Diaspora.

We know that it took the international community thirty years to heed the call made by the oppressed of South Africa. The urgent question, then, is how long the world will tolerate Israel's blatant racism.

The latest BDS successes are, in fact, what we have been calling for since 2005. But we, residents of Gaza, are unable to fathom how it is that, despite Israel's ethnic cleansing and the latest war crimes committed against us, which are well documented by major human rights organizations, and despite Israel's colonization and apartheid, companies and international institutions still carry on business as usual with Israel.

Hasn't it become crystal clear, after all these years and thousands of reports by mainstream human rights organizations, that millions of Palestinians are denied their basic human rights, including the full right to education, free movement, work, and health? We are deprived of a normal life because of more than six hundred Israeli checkpoints, the medieval siege of Gaza, and the apartheid-like discrimination faced by Palestinian citizens of Israel.

We believe that it is our right to expect people of conscience to join us in our struggle against Israeli apartheid by boycotting this intransigent, racist, and militarized Israeli regime and the institutions that keep it thriving. We, Palestinians, are an oppressed people without a state. We increasingly rely on international law and solidarity for our very survival.

What we want is the implementation of international law, an end to the Israeli military occupation of Arab lands occupied in 1967, an end to the policy of colonization and apartheid as practised by Israel against the indigenous population of Palestine of 1948, and the return of Palestinian refugees who were ethnically cleansed in 1948. This is not a call for the end of the state of Israel; it is a call for the end of the ugliest forms of racism. This should be the objective of every person that believes in basic democratic principles.

I believe the BDS movement is the best way to accomplish this. The BDS movement is intended to help secure the democratic rights of the Palestinian people as a whole. We strongly believe that the struggles of the Palestinian people whether as citizens of Israel or in the occupied West Bank and Gaza Strip, and even in the Diaspora, are inseparable. This is the rights-based alternative to the facade of Oslo, which was a "peace" based on the normalization of apartheid. It can provide all Palestinians with a solution that guarantees peace and justice, namely the right of return and equality. Only then can Gaza be transformed from a ghetto surrounded by trigger-happy soldiers and snipers to a beautiful coastal enclave open for citizens of the world to visit, to enjoy its rich, ancient, and multicultural history, the same way people are enjoying the beaches and natural reserves of multiracial South Africa.

The implementation of nonviolent measures, including mass mobilization and a global BDS campaign, should be maintained until apartheid Israel recognizes the Palestinian people's inalienable right to self-determination and the establishment of a democratic state in Mandatory Palestine—a state for all its citizens. We will only then be able to rehumanize Gaza after decades of dehumanization at the hands of Zionist bigots; I will only then be able to drive my car from Gaza to Haifa the same way I drove it from Johannesburg to Cape Town, listening to my favourite Lebanese diva, Fairouz, singing the beautiful lyrics of my favourite poem written by Palestinian poet Haroon Hashem Rashid: *We will return!*

That is our vision of a world without walls.

April 5, 2018

WHAT NEXT FOR GAZA AFTER ISRAEL'S LAND DAY MASSACRE?

After imposing a deadly blockade on the two million inhabitants of the Gaza Strip for eleven years and launching three massive, genocidal attacks in the last seven years—aided by the complicity of the so-called international community and the silence of reactionary Arab regimes—last week, Israel has committed a new massacre against peaceful demonstrators commemorating Land Day and asserting their right of return.*

On Friday, March 30, Israeli soldiers killed seventeen civilians and injured more than fourteen hundred others—mostly with live ammunition. According to the Israeli military, the massacre went according to plan. Their spokesperson tweeted—and later deleted—"[On March 30] nothing was carried out uncontrolled; everything was accurate and measured. We know where every bullet landed."

At the beginning of the second Intifada in 2000, I wrote the following:

> Gaza has become a war zone: the biggest concentration camp on the surface of earth has become a burial site—a noisy graveyard. The Palestinian body has become the ultimate target of the Israeli bullet—the younger the better (Sara, a two-year-old girl from Nablus was also shot in the head.) The Palestinian body has, in other words, become the site of (in)justice: "eliminate the body and it will leave a vacuum that can be occupied—a land without people for people without land."

* Originally published in a slightly different form in Haidar Eid, "What Next for Gaza After Israel's Land Day Massacre?" Opinion, *Al-Jazeera*, April 5, 2018, aljazeera.com. Reprinted with permission from the publisher.

Today, we have a sense of déjà vu; we've been there before and we know that more of us will be killed in what BBC calls "clashes"! The Israeli military, or what the courageous Israeli journalist Gideon Levy calls "the Israel Massacre Forces," are a gang of thugs indoctrinated by an ideology that dehumanizes children and justifies the shooting of innocent civilians.

It is definitely not the right time for such grandiose philosophical questions, but what is the Palestinian to do when he or she lives such a crude political reality?

The question that is on every Gaza Palestinian mind is: Why is this allowed to happen, twenty-four years after the fall of the apartheid regime of South Africa? We do know why Israel is doing it; we are the unwanted "goyim," the refugees whose very existence is a constant reminder of the original sin committed in 1948—the premeditated crime of ethnic cleansing of two-thirds of the Palestinian people. We have been cursed for simply having the "wrong" religion and "ethnicity," for being born to non-Jewish mothers. The problem is that we are not dying quietly; we are making noise, a lot of noise; we are banging the walls of the Gaza tank.

In Gaza, we know that Israel is going to get away with it, simply because it has never been held to account for any of the massacres it has committed; we also know that it is going to commit more and worse crimes.

Hasn't the ESCWA report proven beyond any doubt that Israel is committing the crime of apartheid against the indigenous people of Palestine? We also know that it would not have been able to carry out all these crimes without support from the United States and the so-called international community. We, therefore, have lost hope in official bodies such as the Arab League and the Organisation of Islamic Cooperation. Instead, we are counting on international civil society to put an end to this ongoing bloodbath committed by apartheid Israel in broad day light.

Forget about meaningless negotiations that have proven to be disastrous, as the late Edward Said had rightly predicted back in 1994; forget about the racist two-state solution that has been shot in the head by Israel itself and that fails to deal with the core of the Palestinian question, namely, six to seven million refugees insisting on asserting their UN-stipulated right of return. The only window of hope, in addition to our own mass mobilization, lies in the growing BDS campaign supported by conscious people all over the world. They understand that our struggle is nonsectarian, one that is enshrined in the basic principles of the International Declaration of Human Rights, no matter how hard hypocritical Western media tries to conceal the truth.

April 12, 2018

STANDING UP TO APARTHEID

Contextualizing the Great March of Return

In the last ten years, Israel has launched three massive genocidal wars of aggression on the occupied Gaza Strip, many of our civilians were massacred by its indiscriminate bombing, condemned by UN experts and leading human rights organizations as war crimes and "possible" crimes against humanity.* These assaults left over 3,800 Palestinians dead, predominantly civilians, of whom hundreds were children. Another 15,000 Palestinians were injured. We, the two million Palestinians in the besieged Gaza Strip, the overwhelming majority of whom are refugees who were violently expelled and dispossessed from our homes by Zionist forces in 1948, were subjected to three weeks (2009), two weeks (2012), and fifty-one days (2014) of relentless Israeli state terror, whereby Israeli warplanes systematically targeted civilian areas, reduced whole neighbourhoods and vital civilian infrastructure to rubble, and destroyed scores of schools, including several run by United Nations Relief and Works Agency (UNRWA), where civilians were taking shelter. This came after years of an ongoing, crippling, deadly medieval Israeli siege of Gaza, a severe form of collective punishment described by Richard Falk, former UN special rapporteur for human rights, as "a prelude to genocide."

To understand the mentality behind the killings of tens of civilians, including children, taking place on Gaza borders, all one has to do is read Israel's generals' and politicians' responses. Israeli Defence Minister Avigdor Lieberman said there were "no innocent people" in the Gaza Strip, after Israeli soldiers shot and killed thirty-two Palestinians during ten days of nonviolent, peaceful protests

* Originally published in a slightly different form in Haidar Eid, "Contextualizing the Great March of Return," *Mondoweiss*, April 12, 2018, mondoweiss.net. Reprinted with permission from the publisher.

of refugees demanding the implementation of UN Resolution 194, which calls for their right of return and repatriation and an end to the eleven-year deadly siege. Lieberman claimed that "everyone's connected to Hamas, everyone gets a salary from Hamas."

One cannot but reread a statement made by Israel's ex-deputy defence minister in 2008, Matan Vilnai, who told Army Radio that "[Palestinians of Gaza] will bring upon themselves a bigger shoah because we will use all our might to defend ourselves."

This is a mentality driven by a bigoted ideology that does not see the humanity of the Other let alone their right to self-determination and freedom. They are "two-legged beasts," (Menachem Begin) and "grasshoppers" that have to be crushed after all (Yitzhak Shamir).

And as if eleven years of blockade, interrupted by three genocidal wars, is not enough! The attack on Gaza is not yet over: the Palestinians of Gaza are still living with their physical, mental, and emotional wounds. Their bodies cannot heal because the medicine that is required is not allowed into the Gaza Strip. Their homes cannot be rebuilt and the mangled steel and concrete cannot be removed because the trucks and bulldozers that can remove them are not allowed into the Gaza Strip. Never before has a population been denied the basic requirements for survival as a deliberate policy of colonization, occupation, and apartheid, but this is what Israel is doing to us, the people of Gaza, today: two million people, almost half children under the age of fifteen, live without a secure supply of water, food, electricity, medicines.

It is an "incremental genocide" of the kind unparalleled in human history.

No wonder, then, that leading anti-apartheid activists, the likes of Ronnie Kasrils, ex-South African intelligence minister and member of the ANC, the late Ahmed Kathrada, an ANC leader and Robben Island inmate with Nelson Mandela, and Nobel Peace Laureate Archbishop Desmond Tutu, believe that what Israel is doing to the Palestinians is far worse than what was done to Black South Africans under apartheid. Even former American President Jimmy Carter, on his visit to Gaza, stated clearly that the Palestinian people trapped in Gaza are being treated "like animals."

We are fed up!

We have reached the conclusion that our fight on the ground through a series of marches culminating on May 15, the seventieth anniversary of the Nakba, can pose a serious challenge to Israel's system of occupation, colonization, and apartheid if it is accompanied by a global BDS campaign. We do need ordinary citizens of the world to show Israel that we have a common humanity; that they watch what it does and they will not tolerate it because silence is complicity; that there is no place for their kind of war mongering and barbarism in the world; and that the people of the world reject it. This is exactly what the global anti-apartheid managed to do in the 1970s and 80s until the inhumane apartheid system crumbled. It is time to stand up to the only remaining apartheid regime in the world; for that we need to be united.

May 14, 2018

ON THE SEVENTIETH ANNIVERSARY OF THE NAKBA

Reflections of a Palestinian Refugee

I will not only confine my deliberations to abstract concepts and theories, but I will evoke the reality as we experience and understand it on the ground in Gaza and in the Diaspora.* We Palestinians are fully aware of the fact that we are the victims of an historic issue that has impacted the lives of many and has polarized the discourse on international peace and security.

But what we have learned from the history of state making is that it is not easy to maintain a state that is founded and based upon a historical injustice and the denial of universal freedoms. The history of states is littered with examples of people using all sorts of means of resistance in defence of their universal human rights and fundamental freedoms. We Palestinians are deprived of both. Hence our decades-long multifaceted resistance: armed struggle, popular resistance, BDS, etc.

Eight years ago, I wrote a piece in which I quoted Article I of the Universal Declaration of Human Rights, which states that "All human beings are born free and equal in dignity and rights." It does not, however, say "with the exception of Palestinians." But we, twelve million Palestinians, know very well that we are the exception to that rule. Whether we are Palestinian citizens of Israel, West Bankers and Gazans, or Diasporic refugees, we are not allowed to expect to have the same rights as those of "all human beings."

Any attempt to understand the rationale behind what is essentially a case of blatant violation of fundamental human rights is

* Originally published in a slightly different form in Haidar Eid, "On the 70th Anniversary of the Nakba: Reflections of a Palestinian Refugee," *OpenDemocracy*, May 14, 2018, opendemocracy.net. Reprinted with permission from the publisher.

faced with accusations of anti-Semitism, a weapon used to silence voices calling for justice in the Middle East.

I am convinced that the possibility of having a just peace is today far from realization because of the hermetic medieval siege imposed on more than two million already impoverished people in Gaza and the slicing of the already sliced West Bank. The impossibility of realizing the national dream of one-third of the Palestinian people has brought forward the embarrassing question about the rights of the remaining two-thirds, namely the dispossessed refugees living in miserable camps in other countries and the second-class citizens of the state of Israel.

What is the Palestinian cause if not the right of return of the refugees?

We never tire of asking the question raised by the Nakba generation, the generation that was supposed to die while we are supposed to forget: What is the Palestinian cause if not the right of return of the refugees, those inside and outside Palestine? Can genuine peace be achieved without resolving this?

We live in a world that promotes democratic systems of government. It is supposed to be a system that brings about political stability within a state, that guarantees equality of citizenship and individual freedoms. Nevertheless, the basic tenets of this system of majority rule are tested in multiracial, multireligious, multiethnic, and multicultural societies.

There is an inherent contradiction between advocating democracy as a universal idea while defining the state of Israel in mono-ethnic terms. This approach has only resulted in the relegation of Palestinians residing within the state of Israel to the status of second-class citizens. This undermines, inter alia, the very principle of equal citizenship that is at the core of a democratic system of government.

Zionism is based on the idea of separation, rejection of difference, and ethno-religious supremacy; it is based on a dogma that proclaims that Jews all over the world constitute one nation. In Zionist consciousness, we, native Palestinians, exactly like Native Americans, became a surplus population that must be gotten rid of.

Those who remain would be considered a minority without political and national rights. We, native Palestinians, were viewed by hegemonic Zionism as an obstacle to realizing the Zionist dream by our mere existence and presence. This might explain the continuing ethnic cleansing in the West Bank and the incremental genocide taking place in Gaza.

Like any settler-colonial power, Zionism views native Palestinians as an Other* to be fought against. The Palestinian resistance, peaceful or otherwise, is thus viewed as "criminal violence," "illegitimate," "terrorism," and the list goes on.

The realization of the Zionist dream has meant redemption for some Jews at the expense of the native Palestinians who were dispossessed and relegated to what Fredric Jameson, in another context calls, "the political unconscious."[23] Thus, from the Palestinian perspective, the crystallization of the Zionist dream has meant dispossession and Ghurba.†

Zionism wanted us to be forgotten forever in the political unconscious. However, massacres, humiliation, dispossession, defeat, expropriation, invasion, denial of existence, and now a medieval, hermetic siege . . . have not led to our "disappearance." We have been robbed of our land, deprived of our identity and history; even our future has been stolen. The Zionist response to these atrocities is that the Palestinians should not have existed in the first place. We must remain invisible!

Israel's "independence" has meant a disaster for the Palestinians, who have become the victims of the victims. The goal of Zionism has always been to make us invisible, faceless, and voiceless refugees from nowhere, removed from the world's active consciousness. We had "no history," "no consciousness," "no culture," and thus no story to tell. We, Palestinians are native aliens who became foreigners by the misfortune of being born to non-Jewish mothers.

It is always frustrating that so many activists have no clue about the basics of the Palestinian question. I am always surprised to find myself explaining how, contrary to what has been central in modern liberal thinking, the idea of the citizen in Israel is totally missing. Israel is a state where citizenship and nationality are two

* goy in Hebrew.

† exile

separate, independent concepts. In other words, Israel is not the state of its citizens but the state of the Jewish people. Moreover, Israel does not have a constitution. Since Judaism is a religion, and since it is the basis of the existence of a "modern state," couldn't Islam, Christianity, or Hinduism make the same claim?

Many of us think that the only solution to bring this horror, caused by a settler-colonial project implanted in the heart of the Arab world, to an end is through democratic means by de-Zionizing the state of Israel and transforming it into a state for all of its citizens regardless of race, religion, ethnicity, or gender. There are seven million refugees waiting for that moment, and two million of them have already started their long march to freedom along the Gaza eastern and northern fences separating them from the towns and villages from which they were forcefully expelled in 1948. Alas, my parents are not among those marchers, but I am.

May 16, 2018

WHY I MARCHED ON MAY 14 IN GAZA NEAR THE ISRAELI FENCE

No, it was not because "Hamas made me."

I have been going to the Great March of Return in Gaza two to three times a week ever since it started on March 30.* It makes me feel closer to my village of Zarnouqa, which once stood near what used to be the Palestinian city of al-Ramla. Israeli militias ethnically cleansed the area in 1948, expelling tens of thousands of Palestinians, including my parents.

The Great March of Return is the beginning of our long walk to freedom to undo this injustice of 1948.

We march for three reasons. One, we want UN Resolution 194, which calls for the return of all Palestinian refugees to their lands, to be implemented. Two, we want the genocidal siege imposed on Gaza by apartheid Israel to be lifted. Three, we refuse to accept the decision to move the US embassy to occupied Jerusalem.

We, the marchers, belong to all sectors of Palestinian civil society and all spectrums of political organizations. And despite what the Zionist *hasbara*† might have you believe, it wasn't Hamas who "made" us march.

The National Committee of the March has representatives from all Palestinian political organizations, including Fatah, the Popular Front for the Liberation of Palestine, the Democratic Front for the Liberation of Palestine, and the National Initiative, among others.

On May 14, I was one of tens of thousands of Gazans who decided to go to the eastern fence lined with Israeli snipers.

* Originally published in a slightly different form in Haidar Eid, "Why I Marched May 14 in Gaza Near the Israeli Fence," Opinion, *Al-Jazeera*, May 16, 2018, aljazeera.com. Reprinted with permission from the publisher.

† propaganda

"Today will be a grand day in Palestinian history! A day all Palestinians, Arabs and freedom-loving people will remember for ages to come!" I wrote on my Facebook wall just before I left home that day to drive with my three friends—an academic, a salesman, and an activist—to join the march.

There were tens of thousands of people there with us—men, women, and children, entire families from all walks of life.

These thousands of people, walking unarmed to the fence to demand their right to return, worried Israel. Its government gave instructions to the soldiers to shoot any civilian trying to "trespass."

And so the shooting began as early as nine o'clock that morning. I saw women, children, amputees, young men, and elderly get shot, even though they were not trying to "trespass." One young man, whose face I will never forget, was shot in the abdomen and never made it to the hospital.

A young woman, whose face was covered with a Palestinian keffiyeh, was shot in the neck but survived. By the end of the day, we lost 60 people, and more than 2,700 were injured.

The most heartbreaking deaths were those of eight-month-old baby Laila El-Ghandour and Fadi Abu Saleh, an amputee who had lost his legs to an Israeli mine. Two of the sixty martyrs were brothers.

And then, I received the news of the martyrdom of my friend Ahmed al-Udini, who left behind a three-year-old daughter. He was a leftist student activist who, after graduation, joined the BDS group in Gaza and worked as a show presenter at the Al-Shaab radio station. He was no "terror threat," as Israel would have you believe.

As we get ready to bury him and the rest of the dead, we know that we have been abandoned. The bitter reality is that we are alone, beleaguered, under siege, and undesirable even to some of those who are supposed to be our brethren.

For six weeks now, we have faced the onslaught by one of the world's strongest armies, which possesses hundreds of nuclear warheads, more than 150,000 troops on active duty, Merkava battle tanks, F-16 jets, Apache attack helicopters, gunboats, and drones.

When Israel is not sniping us down or bombing us, it exerts

great effort to ensure that we live in subhuman conditions under siege in Gaza. We get electricity for only four hours a day, 95 percent of our water is undrinkable, and our seriously ill wither away as they wait for months for a permit to get treatment in the West Bank.

As our hospitals, already crippled by the siege, are struggling to cope with the twelve thousands injured since March 30, some Arab regimes and a complicit EU are doing absolutely nothing except issuing timid statements. In reality, they have let down the Palestinians for years, and to this day, official international attitudes are a combination of cowardice and hypocrisy.

The international community, the UN, the EU, and Arab leaders have remained largely silent about the atrocities committed by apartheid Israel. Instead, they are asking us to stay quiet in Gaza, the largest open-air concentration camp, so as not to inconvenience the Israeli occupiers.

We are expected to conduct ourselves as "house Palestinians," like the house slaves who were grateful to their white masters and who were satisfied to eat the leftovers from their tables. We are required to accept our slow death and show no form of resistance, to accept that if we get shot, then it is our own fault.

As we are burying our dead, we do know that we have only one tenable option. This option does not entail waiting for the Security Council, the EU, or the Arab League to convene.

This option is "power of the people," the only force capable of facing off with the Israeli military occupation. We have chosen to fight for dignity, a departure from years of self-deception that portrayed slavery under the occupier as a fait accompli.

The result of this decision made by Palestinian civil society and all political forces is the Great March of Return.

The only way forward for us is to follow the same route as the South African struggle. It focused on mobilizing the masses on the ground rather than indifferent governments around the world.

What hope could South Africans have had to get help from the likes of Margaret Thatcher and Ronald Reagan? It was up to ordinary South Africans and global citizens to reject and resist the crimes committed by the ugly apartheid system.

Our main advantage as Palestinians in this unequal fight is what the late Edward Said called "the high moral ground." Our victory at the end will be the inevitable result of our steadfastness, which has not wavered despite the feeling that we have been left on our own.

June 14, 2018

IT IS TIME TO LEVY SANCTIONS AGAINST ISRAEL

Since the beginning of the Great March of Return on March 30, around 120 Palestinians have been killed and more than 13,000 injured, including many children.* About a third of those wounded were hit by live fire from Israeli snipers.

The latest victim of Israeli brutality was twenty-one-year-old Razan al-Najjar, a paramedic murdered by an Israeli sniper hidden in a ditch on the other side of the fence. Razan was shot while she was trying to save a protestor's life.

Every single Palestinian in Gaza knows that Israeli soldiers meant to kill her, considering a tweet on March 30 by the Israeli army spokesperson in which he stated very clearly that "everything was accurate and measure and [they] knew where every bullet landed."

To better understand the gravity, and the horror, of this, note that in fifty-one days of Israel's 2014 war in Gaza, around twelve housand people were injured.

The apartheid state of Israel appears intent on solving its "problem" of the surplus population of native Palestinians in Gaza by maiming most of them, with its forces firing fatal bullets, which are prohibited for use against peaceful demonstrators under international law.

Medieval Blockade

Israel's excuse—as if it ever needs one—is that Palestinians in Gaza are trying to "infiltrate the border," but this idea misrepresents reality.

* Originally published in a slightly different form in Haidar Eid, "It Is Time to Levy Sanctions Against Israel," Opinion, *Middle East Eye*, June 4, 2018, middleeasteye.net. Reprinted with permission from the publisher.

Palestinians in Gaza are not infiltrators; they are people living under occupation and an unprecedented, medieval blockade. Gaza has been turned into what UN human rights chief Zeid Raad al-Hussein calls a "toxic slum."

The slogan of the Great March of Return is "I want to go home." Seventy percent of Palestinians in Gaza are refugees from cities and towns in Israel.

All attempts to prove that Hamas is behind the latest protests are tainted with racism. It is a civil society initiative—and, yes, Palestinians in Gaza do have a vibrant civil society.

Between the growing BDS campaign and the Great March of Return, we aim to see a day when Israeli human rights violations no longer occur with impunity. Empty talk about improving the conditions of our oppression means absolutely nothing because we will continue marching as long as UN Resolution 194 is not implemented and as long as our bodies are confined to this tiny prison called Gaza.

Racist Worldview

Our narrative is rooted in universal principles of human rights, equality, justice, and international law. We understand, like the Black people of South Africa under apartheid and the US African American community, that racist bigots have a problem with that logic, as it does not fit within their racist worldview.

Israel's nightmare is when it has to confront Palestinian advocates who speak with power and credibility about Palestine and debunk misconceptions that attempt to distract the international community from Israel's flagrant human rights violations.

The Gaza massacres have become normalized acts of policy, not individual aberrations. To add insult to injury, the apartheid state of Israel has announced that it will not cooperate with a UN Human Rights Council probe of Gaza deaths. This is a mindset that denies the humanity of the Palestinians of Gaza.

Gilad Erdan, Israel's strategic affairs minister, has referred to innocent Palestinians in Gaza as "Nazis"—not unlike white, racist officers of South Africa's apartheid regime accusing Black Africans of racism. And on May 29, Energy Minister Yuval Steinitz threatened to destroy Gaza, saying: "I do not rule out the possibility of conquering Gaza and destroying it once and for all."

The Israeli government, its ambassadors, and its apologists claim that massacring Palestinians is a way to defend Israeli sovereignty against "terrorists." Every occupying colonial power refers to those opposing the occupation as terrorists. Nelson Mandela was one of those "terrorists" the apartheid regime—and even the likes of former US president Ronald Reagan and former British prime minister Margaret Thatcher—didn't like at all.

BDS: A Window of Hope

Apparently, Israeli soldiers will never forgive us for making them kill us—hence the necessity for BDS, our only window of hope.

It is time for the world to stand up and act—to impose sanctions on Israeli industries until Palestinians are granted freedom, equal civil rights, and justice.

In the 1980s, the world was fed up with the apartheid regime of South Africa and decided to initiate sanctions against it; those sanctions helped to free native Africans from apartheid. It is time for the world to rally behind sanctions on Israel in a similar fashion, until it complies with international law.

The world owes Gaza the mother of all apologies, but all we are asking for is a military embargo on Israel similar to the one imposed on apartheid South Africa, until this racist madness comes to an end.

July 22, 2018

ISRAEL HAS FINALLY COME OUT AS AN ETHNO-RELIGIOUS STATE

In Palestine, we are dealing with a complex situation: We have a settler-colonial project that denies its colonialism and argues it is a democracy, and we have its victims whose victimization has been dismissed for decades and whose national liberation struggle has been defamed.*

The colonizers have been successful in manipulating the narrative on what is going on, rewriting history, and whitewashing their crimes. Various countries around the world have bought into their lies and kept a "neutral" stance, claiming their positions are "balanced."

What is there to balance, when one side has one of the most advanced armies in the world, financed and supplied by an allied superpower, and the other side has been altogether abandoned by allies and well-wishers and has only the determination and strength of its people to rely on?

But these claims of "neutrality" and "balance" are no longer tenable. Israel has stopped playing the democracy pretense game and has revealed itself for what it really is: an apartheid state. On July 19, the Israeli Knesset voted to pass the so-called nation-state law, which declares Israel "the national home of the Jewish people." It is now officially an exclusive ethno-religious state.

Unveiling the Ethno-Religious State of Israel

For us Palestinians, this law reiterates the obvious: namely, that the Zionist ideology is inherently racist and undemocratic.

The political goal of Zionism was to engineer a demographic

* Originally published in a slightly different form in Haidar Eid, "Israel Has Finally Come Out As an Ethno-religious State," Opinion, *Al-Jazeera*, July 22, 2018, aljazeera.com. Reprinted with permission from the publisher.

shift in Palestine, making the minority Jewish population (which was just 7.6 percent in 1914) a majority through massive Jewish immigration and settlement building and expulsion of the Palestinians.

Inevitably, the expropriation of land went hand-in-hand with the violation of rights of the Palestinian majority. Zionists have always looked at Palestinians as invisible if not absent, or rather "present absentees." The identity of those who remained within the boundaries of what was to become Israel was erased through the term "Israeli Arab" and their rights curbed by myriad laws ("the nation-state law" being just the latest iteration).

This is because, contrary to modern liberal thinking, in Israel, citizenship and nationality are two separate, independent concepts. In other words, Israel is not the state of its citizens, but the state of the Jewish people. Thus Palestinians in Israel have Israeli passports, but they do not have rights equal to those of Jewish citizens.

With the new nation-state law, Palestinians in Israel are now considered "native aliens" or foreigners in their own homeland because Israel is defined by its law as " the historical homeland of the Jewish people"; that is, not the state of all of its citizens. This is the direct result of Zionism and its ideology of racism.

It is also the direct result of prevailing undemocratic sentiments among Israel's Jews. The contradiction between professed ideals and actual behaviour, which has been the engine of political change in many places around the world, does not exist in Israel because the democratic creed, or civic democracy, is absent in Israeli society.

There is no promise of equality for all citizens in Israeli political culture and praxis. And there is no tradition of civil liberties in Israel because such a tradition is incompatible with Zionism.

Hence, one can understand the antagonism of the establishment to calls for the creation of one state for Palestinians and Jews, one secular democratic state run by parliamentary elections and majority rule in historical Palestine. This idea has been rejected outright by Israeli Jewish society because it would effectively mean the end of Zionism.

And as Israel effectively turns into an exclusive ethno-religious state, we have to ask uncomfortable questions: Does this mean that Islam, Christianity, Hinduism, etc., can also be the basis of modern states? And if we still insist that religion should be separate from state, then where is the international outrage? Why isn't mainstream media obsessing about the Jewish state, the way it was about the "Islamic state"? How is Israel different from the Islamic State of Iraq and the Levant that sought to establish a state for Muslims only through violence and dispossession?

The Fight Against Apartheid Is On

The passing of the nation-state law should eliminate whatever doubt there still is among "neutral" observers that Israel is, in fact, an apartheid state.

Just as apartheid South Africa gave citizenship to white South Africans and relegated Black South Africans to "independent homelands," Zionism gives all Jews the right to citizenship in the state of Israel, while denying citizenship to Palestinians—its indigenous inhabitants.

While South Africa's apartheid used race to determine citizenship, the state of Israel uses religious identification to determine citizenship. Just as apartheid South Africa made laws criminalizing free movement of Black people on their ancestral land, Israel controls every aspect of Palestinians' lives through a military occupation infrastructure composed of checkpoints, Jewish-only settlements and roads, and the wall,* combined with a web of legal regulations.

The parallels between Israel and apartheid South Africa are infinite. And probably the only major difference between the two is that Israel gets away with its crimes with unprecedented impunity, as evidenced by its latest war crimes in Gaza.

So what is left for the Palestinian people after the approval of this blatantly racist bill? Well, we definitely are not foolish enough to expect anything from the so-called international community.

Years of "negotiations" created only Bantustans in the West Bank and a concentration camp in Gaza. Palestinians are still at

* The wall, 708 km of concrete and fences built by Israel to contain Palestinians in their designated territories, is an illegal structure that has been condemned by the UN, the ICJ, and many other human rights organizations.

the receiving end of merciless assaults by racist Israeli troops hidden in their US-made helicopters and F-16s.

What all US envoys to the region have been trying to do is reach a "solution" in accordance with Israeli conditions, disregarding Security Council resolutions and international law. Neither the current US right-wing administration nor the spineless EU has a fair plan for how to resolve the crisis in Palestine.

The only thing that we, Palestinians, can count on is the power of people, just as South Africans did when, through a sustained global campaign, they forced governments to boycott their apartheid regime.

We will continue to expand the BDS movement and to march to the fence in Gaza until we bring this madness to an end. We will also continue working on an alternative model, both democratic and secular, that guarantees equality and abolishes apartheid, Bantustans, and separation in Palestine altogether. We will not give up the fight.

July 24, 2018

BACK TO THE FUTURE

The Great March of Return

The Great March of Return—which began on March 30 and has not yet ended—has shuffled the cards and brought crucial questions to the fore regarding the essence of the Palestinian cause as well as the status of the Gaza Strip.* Despite the bleak reality of life in Gaza, which Israel's siege will, with international and local collusion, soon render uninhabitable, a new awareness is emerging.

This new awareness is undercutting the long-dominant policies of the current right-wing leadership and the superficial "opposition" represented by what I call the Stalinist Left—that is, both the Popular and Democratic Fronts for the Liberation of Palestine, the Palestinian People's Party, the Palestinian Democratic Union and, to some extent, the Palestinian National Initiative. These parties have so far failed to emerge from their intellectual subordination to the now defunct Soviet Union and continue to depend financially on the right-wing leadership of the Palestinian Liberation Organization. In other words, they rely on the PA for their existence and are unable to forge independent and effective strategies.

Given the failure of the dominant political class after seventy years of displacement and dispossession since the Nakba, eleven years of blockade that international human rights organizations have described as a crime against humanity, and three Israeli wars that have killed more than four thousand men, women, and children, the Palestinians of Gaza have decided to peacefully mobilize to enforce international resolutions, beginning with UN Resolution 194 regarding the return of Palestinian refugees to their homes and lands.

* Originally published in a slightly different form in Haidar Eid, "Back to the Future: The Great March of Return," *Al-Shabaka*, July 24, 2018, al-shabaka.org. Reprinted with permission from the publisher.

Indeed, as Gaza-based civil society and political activists have concluded, the only dependable power is that of the people, especially after the Palestinian leadership turned its back on the Gaza Strip and began to impose punitive measures against it in April 2017. The struggle against apartheid in South Africa has inspired Palestinian activists since the late 1980s and the popular mobilization of the First Intifada. Palestinian activists also draw on a history of popular resistance in Palestine, including the 1936 strike and later uprisings in the West Bank, Gaza Strip, and Israel.

Activists Have Concluded the Only Dependable Power Is That of the People

The new awareness emerging in and from Gaza connects all forms of popular resistance. In particular, it upholds the call to boycott, divest from, and impose sanctions on Israel, inspired by the South African liberation movement. Indeed, the March of Return has created an unprecedented Palestinian consensus and is in line with the goals of the BDS movement. BDS activists have participated in the march from the very beginning, holding awareness-raising events in partnership with organizers of the march in which they have shown the direct relationship between the main forms of popular resistance and the role of civil society in taking the lead in these forms, given the lessons of past experience and approaches such as armed resistance.

The Gaza March of Return campaign has the potential to promote true national unity after all the attempts to reconcile Fatah and Hamas since 2006 have failed. All the political parties are participating in the march and have representatives on the High National Committee alongside civil society representatives. The fact that both Hamas and Fatah have representatives on this committee demonstrates that only political activists directly connected to the people can achieve what party leaders have failed to accomplish. And party leaders have failed because the present Palestinian political system represents class and group interests that depend on internal divisions to survive, as well as on security coordination with Israel's occupation. The march has proven that a wide gap separates the Palestinian leadership from the Palestinian people, especially those in Gaza.

The new awareness created by the Great March of Return is also apparent in the complete break with the Oslo process and its vision of a mini-state alongside a Jewish state that practices racism against its own people. It has the potential to revive the concepts of national liberation and self-determination by addressing the new facts on the ground that Israel created. These realities have rendered it impossible to establish an independent, sovereign Palestinian state on 22 percent of the land of historic Palestine. Therefore, the time has come for a decisive struggle for freedom, equality, and justice. After all, two-thirds of Gaza residents are refugees whose rights to both return and reparations are guaranteed by international law.

The BDS movement has not embraced a clear political stance on the question of statehood or whether there should be two states or a single democratic state. However, the March of Return's goals fly in the face of the two-state solution since it is essentially in contradiction with the main demand of marchers, that is, the return and reparation of refugees. The holding of sister marches in Haifa, Ramallah, Bethlehem, and Umm Al-Fahm highlights the pan-Palestinian nature of the March of Return and its spread from the besieged Gaza Strip to the OPT and Israel. And this is exactly what worries Israel.

This popular initiative is an attempt to redirect efforts towards achieving legitimate rights and to interconnect the three segments of the Palestinian people—the Palestinian citizens of Israel and Palestinians in the OPT and the Diaspora. It also proves that Gaza constitutes an integral part of Palestinian national identity. Palestinians in Gaza have never been unpatriotic and cannot be held responsible for the deep national rift. They have played a vital role in shaping and vigorously defending modern Palestinian nationalism, which is precisely what the march has affirmed.

The March of Return's Goals Fly in the Face of the Two-State Solution

The Palestinian leadership has now submitted a referral to the International Criminal Court (ICC) claiming that Israeli officials committed war crimes and crimes against humanity against the Palestinian people. Palestinian leaders must go further: they must renounce the constraints of Oslo, including security coordination and economic subordination, and unequivocally embrace the BDS movement's call. They should not enter any "negotiations" unless the implementation of Resolution 194 tops the agenda. They must ensure that any negotiations tackle the demand to end the apartheid policies against Palestinian citizens of Israel.

Finally, the struggle for freedom, return, and self-determination for all segments of the Palestinian people is the concrete embodiment of inclusive national unity on the ground. This unity is not defined by two political factions, or by the so-called two parts of the homeland (that is, the West Bank and Gaza), but rather by the new collective awareness to which the March of Return and the BDS movement have contributed.

August 3, 2018

ISRAEL'S POLICIES IN GAZA ARE GENOCIDAL

The 1948 Genocide Convention clearly states that one instance of genocide is "the deliberate infliction of conditions of life calculated to bring about the physical destruction of a people in whole or in part."* No matter whether this happens quickly or in "slow motion." That is what has been done to Gaza since the imposition of the blockade by Israel and the subsequent massacres, which led to the death of more than four thousand Palestinians in three successive genocidal wars.

Palestinians of Gaza live an ongoing, illegal, crippling Israeli siege that has shattered all spheres of life, prompting the former UN Special Rapporteur for Human Rights Richard Falk to describe it as "a prelude to genocide." In 2009, the UN Fact-Finding Mission on the Gaza Conflict, headed by the highly respected South African judge Richard Goldstone, found Israel guilty of "war crimes and possible crimes against humanity," as did major international human rights organizations, such as Amnesty International and Human Rights Watch. The Goldstone Report, for example, concludes that Israel's war on Gaza was "designed to punish, humiliate and terrorize a civilian population, radically diminish its local economic capacity both to work and to provide for itself, and to force upon it an ever increasing sense of dependency and vulnerability."

The same scenario was repeated in 2012, and a worse one in 2014, only because Israel feels that it can carry on its war crimes with full impunity. And last week, Israel decided to tighten the siege by closing the only commercial crossing and even to increase its attacks by targeting peaceful protestors demanding

* Originally published in a slightly different form in Haidar Eid, "Israel's Policies in Gaza Are Genocidal," *Mondoweiss*, August 3, 2018, mondoweiss.net. Reprinted with permission from the publisher.

the implementation of UN resolutions and an end to this deadly, hermetic siege.

In her visit to Gaza, Professor Sara Roy, an expert on Gaza, describes the Strip as "a land ripped apart and scarred, the lives of its people blighted. Gaza is decaying under the weight of continued devastation, unable to function normally." Professor Roy concludes, "The decline and disablement of Gaza's economy and society have been deliberate, the result of state policy–consciously planned, implemented and enforced . . . And just as Gaza's demise has been consciously orchestrated, so have the obstacles preventing its recovery." In addition to Israel's daily attacks and air strikes, Gazans also suffer from the contamination of water, air, and soil, since the sewage system is unable to function due to power cuts necessitated by a lack of fuel to the main generators of the Gaza power grid. Medical conditions due to injuries from internationally prohibited butterfly bullets and other illegal Israeli weapons as well as from water contamination cannot be treated because of the siege. In addition to the ban on building materials, Israel also prevents many other necessities from being imported: light bulbs, candles, matches, books, refrigerators, shoes, clothing, mattresses, sheets, blankets, tea, coffee, sausages, flour, cows, pasta, cigarettes, fuel, pencils, pens, paper, etc. In Gaza, people are wondering whether the current Israeli government, the most fascist in the county's history, might even discuss a ban on oxygen! Add to this the punitive measure taken by the PA, and the drastic cuts endorsed by UNRWA, not to mention the constant closure of the Rafah crossing—the only exit Gaza has to the external world—leading to some of the highest rates of unemployment and poverty on the face of the earth.

In fact, the conclusion Gazans have reached is that Israel is intent on destroying Gaza because world official bodies and leaders choose to say and do absolutely nothing. The brazen refusal of Israel to cooperate with the decision of the international community to reconstruct Gaza, for which several billions of dollars were pledged in Sharm El-Sheikh, should not be tolerated. Israel's attacks have damaged or completely destroyed many public buildings and have, according to the UN's own Office for the Coordination of Humanitarian Affairs reports, severely damaged or completely destroyed some thousands of family dwellings, schools, universities, and factories. Many other Palestinians who have spent the past several winters and summers in tents and caravans have also been promised the means to rebuild homes and schools, though to date nothing has been done to alleviate their suffering.

The practice of wanton, wilful killing of civilians exemplified in the extrajudicial sniping of nonviolent protestors at the eastern fence of the Gaza Strip is not an isolated incident. It is part and parcel of an ongoing, comprehensive policy targeting the civilian Palestinians of the Gaza Strip and systematically denying them their rights to movement, work, medical care, study, livelihood, and, increasingly, life itself. But it is also a reflection of the nature of the state of Israel; that is, a settler colony led by an exclusionary, genocidal ideology; a settler-colonial movement that is interested in having as much of the land of Palestine with as few Palestinians on it as possible. The late scholar of settler colonialism Patrick Wolfe maintained that the encounter between the settlers and the indigenous population triggered "the logic of the elimination of the native."[24]

In spite of Israel's alleged unilateral withdrawal from the Strip in 2005, it still maintains a permanent military presence in Gaza's territorial waters and controls the movement of people and goods onto the Strip by land and water in addition to movement within the Strip through targeting anyone entering the "no go" zone designated by the Israeli military. Israel also continues to control Gaza's population registry. Yet, Israel claims that it is no longer the occupying power in the Gaza Strip and uses this excuse, in addition to the results of 2006 democratic elections, to intensify its policy of siege and lethal attacks on Gaza's civilians.

And now, Israel has decided to become an openly apartheid state by legalizing racial discrimination. I have tried very hard to find out whether there are constitutions or laws in the world similar to Israel's "new" Nation-State Basic Law, which aims to establish a legal basis for Jewish supremacy and racism against indigenous Palestinians, including those living in what has become the largest open-air prison on earth; only South Africa under apartheid and America in the eras of slavery and segregation.

So, what to do?!

In a piece published in *Middle East Eye*, Gideon Levy asks, "Israel, where is your outrage at the legislation of Apartheid?"[25] Actually, we are not expecting a settler-colonial community to act against its own racism. The outside world has to intervene. Hence our call for BDS. But, in Palestine, we are in urgent need of serious discussions about a program of radical political transformation, what with the disastrous failure of the existing programs, Right and Left, a program that divorces itself from the racist two-state solution, one that endorses a more inclusive program that guarantees the rights of all segments of the Palestinian people.

October 12, 2018

FRAGMENTED THOUGHTS FROM THE EASTERN FENCE OF THE GAZA OPEN-AIR PRISON

I am writing this piece after returning from one of the marches today at the eastern fence of the Gaza concentration camp, where 6 young men have been brutally shot dead and more than 112 injured by Israeli snipers. Sources from the Palestinian Ministry of Health are telling me that the number is expected to rise.

Zionism originated as a racist colonial movement with the agenda to ethnically cleanse the land of Palestine of its indigenous population in order to set up an exclusively Jewish state at the expense of the Palestinian people.* History has proven that if unchecked, this agenda also allows Zionism to pose a dangerous threat beyond Palestine's borders to the rest of the Arab world. The Zionist terror against us includes the continuation of ethnic cleansing and racism in the land of Palestine, sentencing surviving Palestinians to a life in exile in different parts of the world.

Our present focus on a constructive program for Palestinian liberation is based first and foremost on our insistence on the right of return to our national homeland, primarily as a natural right and secondly as a right enforced by international law. For this reason, it is not surprising that Palestinian nationalism is being carried on the shoulders of the sons of the refugee camps, those who have taught themselves through their experience of the reality of being refugees that they must insist upon recognizing and rejecting this reality. They are the sons and daughters of those who will return, not those who are refugees.

* Originally published in a slightly different form in Haidar Eid, "Fragmented Thoughts from the Eastern Fence of the Gaza Open-Air Prison," *Mondoweiss*, October 12, 2018, mondoweiss.net. Reprinted with permission from the publisher.

Therefore, it is not surprising that our fellow Palestinians who remained within the 1948 borders have lifted up their banners to insist that they are there to stay, clinging to the right of return. Nothing can obstruct this vision of a people determined on life, despite the short sightedness of the US and complicit EU.

The demand for the right of return has been and will always be the focal point of Palestinian self-determination, with the wishes of the whole of the Palestinian people, having justice and democracy on their side in facing Zionism, as a purely exclusivist ideology. We must ask uncomfortable questions: How did things become so distorted in this historical confrontation faced by the Palestinian people? In the South African context, the equation was clear. It is mind-boggling! In fact, it is so absurd that we continue to be burdened by this kind of questions about ourselves.

We see that the answer lies within the Palestinian concessions, which reached their culmination in the 1993 Oslo Accords. The Oslo Declaration showed the capitulation of the essence of freedom and self-determination for Palestinian liberation and allowed the page of "terrorism" to be attached in fabrication. The negotiation for the right of return was merged into a discussion of the institutions of self-government, which would be called a "state." This complicity involved the deception of a "two state solution" as a cover to settle the issue of Palestinian nationalism and the rights of the Palestinian people.

All this indicates that there is a need to absolutely refuse the fate drawn for us by Israeli and American right-wing governments. There is also an urgent need to work politically to offer an alternative to this reality, instead of searching for alternatives that have not only proved to be delusional but threaten our very existence.

The final judgment is approaching. Either exist or be wiped out from history. Therefore, it is the moment of truth; either be steadfast during this certainly delusional settlement, the settlement of a state, a Bantustan, with partial authority over the Palestinian people, or the delusion of a settlement under Israeli citizenship, regardless of the right of return. We, marchers at the eastern fence of the Gaza Ghetto, beg to differ! We want the full menu of rights or nothing!

November 9, 2018

WHAT GAZA WANTS

As we, Palestinians of Gaza, embark on our long walk to freedom, we have come to the conclusion that we can no longer rely on governments; instead, we request that the citizens of the world oppose these ongoing deadly crimes.* The failure of the United Nations and its numerous organizations to condemn such crimes proves their complicity. We have also come to the conclusion that only civil society is able to mobilize to demand the implementation of international law and put an end to Israel's unprecedented impunity. Our inspiration is the anti-apartheid movement. The intervention of civil society was effective in the late 1980s against the apartheid regime of white South Africa. Nelson Mandela, before his eminent death, and Archbishop Desmond Tutu, among other anti-apartheid activists, not only described Israel's oppressive and violent control of Palestinians as apartheid, they also joined this call for the world's civil society to intervene again.

In fact, we expect people of conscience and civil society organizations to put pressure on their governments until Israel is forced to abide by international law and international humanitarian law. It did work last century; without the intervention of the international community, which was effective against apartheid in South Africa, Israel will continue its war crimes and crimes against humanity.

We need to be more specific about our demands. We want civil society organizations worldwide to intensify the anti-Israel sanctions campaign to compel Israel to end to its aggression.

It has become crystal clear that the international conspiracy of silence towards the incremental genocide taking place

* Originally published in a slightly different form in Haidar Eid, "What Gaza Wants," *Mondoweiss*, November 9, 2018, mondoweiss.net. Reprinted with permission from the publisher.

against the two million civilians in Gaza indicates complicity in these war crimes.

It is high-time the international community demand that the rogue state of Israel, a state that has violated every single international law one can think of, end its medieval siege of Gaza and compensate for the destruction of life and infrastructure that it has visited upon the Palestinian people. But this should also come within a package of demands to be made by all Palestine solidarity groups and all international civil society organizations that still believe in the rule of law and basic human rights:

- An end to the siege that has been imposed on the Palestinians of the Gaza Strip since 2006 for voting against the fictional two-state solution and the Oslo Accords.
- The protection of civilian lives and property, as stipulated in International Humanitarian Law and International Human Rights Law such as the Fourth Geneva Convention.
- That Palestinian refugees in the Gaza Strip be provided with material support to cope with the immense hardship they are experiencing at the hands of Israeli occupation forces.
- Immediate reparations and compensation for all destruction carried out by the Israeli Occupation Forces (IOF) in the Gaza Strip.
- Holding Israeli generals and leaders accountable for war crimes and crimes against humanity committed against the civilians of Gaza.
- An end to occupation, apartheid, and other war crimes committed by Israel.

Why is that too much to ask? Were the anti-apartheid and civil rights movements too demanding for calling for an end to all forms of racism, institutional and otherwise? And was the international community wrong to heed their calls?

May 6, 2019

GAZA HAS MADE ITS CHOICE

It Will Continue to Resist

We have spent sleepless nights under Israeli bombs before—in 2006, 2008, 2012, 2014, and 2018.* On Saturday, apartheid Israel decided to launch yet another murderous campaign of bombardment against one of the most densely populated areas on earth.

Again, the victims were children and women. Fourteen-month-old Palestinian toddler Siba Abu Arrar was killed, along with her pregnant aunt, Falastine, who succumbed to her wounds shortly after American-made, Israeli warplanes targeted their home in Zeitoun neighbourhood.

On Friday, like all the previous fifty-seven Fridays, I joined thousands of peaceful protestors at the eastern fence of the Gaza concentration camp, where Israeli snipers shot and killed four Palestinians and injured fifty-one, including children. One of those killed was nineteen-year-old Raed Abu Teir, who was walking on crutches, having been injured during previous protests.

Calls for a ceasefire were made as Israel's Prime Minister Benjamin Netanyahu vowed to launch "massive strikes" in the hope of killing the largest possible number of Palestinians by targeting residential areas.

As with previous truce initiatives, this time once again Israel and the Palestinians—the oppressor and the oppressed—were equated as "two sides to a conflict," and what constitutes legitimate resistance under international law was put on the same level as a brutal illegal occupation. The fact that Israel has an actual army, disproportionately bigger firepower, and is an occupier was

* Originally published in a slightly different form in Haidar Eid, "Gaza Has Made Its Choice: It Will Continue to Resist," Opinion, *Al-Jazeera*, May 6, 2019, aljazeera.com. Reprinted with permission from the publisher.

neglected as usual, and so was the stark difference in the death toll: twenty-four Palestinians and four Israelis.

Like all previous ceasefires mediated by the Egyptian authorities and the United Nations, this one also aimed to maintain "stability" in the open-air concentration camp that Gaza is, for as long as possible, by demanding that any form of resistance is subdued.

In this case, the Israeli government is eager to quiet Gaza down ahead of the generous opportunity European countries are giving it to whitewash its war crimes by hosting the Eurovision song contest in Tel Aviv, an hour's drive away from the Strip.

As in the past, Palestinians are now expected to gratefully accept a "period of calm," where Israeli bombs are not raining on their houses and its blockade continues to strangulate Gaza.

In fact, what has come to be regularly required of the Palestinians is to conduct themselves as "house Palestinians" and be thankful to their white Ashkenazi masters for the breadcrumbs they let them have in order to barely survive.

They are to give in to a slow death, die like cockroaches, showing no form of rebellion, and accept that if they die resisting, then it would be their own fault.

Palestinians will no longer accept the dictates of the so-called international community that continues to favour Israel and cover up its war crimes. Any talk of improving the conditions of oppression in light of the great sacrifices made by our people is a betrayal of Palestinian victims.

Any ceasefire agreement that does not lead to the immediate lifting of the blockade on the Gaza Strip and the reopening of the Rafah crossing, and all the other crossings, in a manner that allows the inflow of fuel, medicine, and all other basic goods and does not include provisions for ending the Israeli occupation and apartheid—will not be accepted.

We will no longer allow Gaza to be severed from Palestine and the historical context behind the suffering of its people. This is not a "conflict," as the Israelis like to present it, with a hostile armed group.

It is an occupation, launched by a settler-colonial power that seeks to ethnically cleanse an entire indigenous population in order to solidify and legitimize its colony. What is happening in Gaza is incremental genocide, not a "security operation."

The barbaric massacres committed by apartheid Israel since 2006 have claimed the lives of thousands of Palestinians, the majority of them civilians, including many children. Entire families have been wiped out in broad daylight in conjunction with the systematic destruction of hundreds of Palestinian homes; doctors and paramedics were killed while on duty and so were journalists. Tens of thousands have been permanently disabled in these wars.

We, the Palestinians in Gaza, have already made our choice. We will not die a dishonourable slow death while thanking our killers under the self-deception that portrays slavery to the occupier as a fait accompli.

No, we will continue to fight for our dignity, for ourselves, and for our children. We, members of the Palestinian civil society, have long argued that the way forward should be people's power—the only force capable of tackling the huge asymmetry of power in the struggle against Israel.

And our Great March of Return has demonstrated this. We successfully broke efforts to intentionally separate the Gaza "conflict" from its roots and made our demands heard across the world. We don't want another short-term ceasefire or slight "improvement" in living conditions under a "deal of the century." We don't want breadcrumbs. We want to return to our lands, we want our rights under international law to be recognized.

That is why, each Friday, we continue to call for boycott, divestment, and sanctions against Israel and we hail the effort of various groups and individuals across the world—the true international community—who have joined our efforts.

We now call on all Eurovision artists to give up their participation in whitewashing the murder of toddlers, pregnant women, medics, journalists, and musicians and the destruction of civilian homes, hospitals, schools, and cultural centres.

Do you really want to entertain Israeli soldiers sniping down unarmed protestors? Do you really want to perform sixty kilometres away from Gaza, where the family of the fourteen-month-old Siba cannot stop grieving? Do you really want to sing in apartheid Israel?

It is time for you, as well as the rest of the art world, to stand on the right side of history—just like they did a few decades ago during the apartheid era in South Africa—and boycott Israel.

November 20, 2019

THE ONLY REMAINING HOPE IN GAZA IS KNOWING THIS NIGHTMARE CAN BE BROUGHT TO AN END

The latest round of alleged Israeli war crimes in Gaza has resulted in a new massacre in the besieged Gaza Strip.* Thirty-four people including four families and eight children were murdered as they slept in their own houses within forty-eight hours. More than a hundred have been critically injured. The scenes of the amputated bodies of the Abu Malhous family are etched into our psyche for generations to come. We will tell our remaining children about this heinous massacre the same way our parents and grandparents told us about the Deir Yassin massacre.

But will this nightmare come to an end?

One question foreign journalists keep asking me is about Israel's endgame, its strategy after keeping Gaza on life support since 2007. I assume Black South Africans were never asked about the apartheid regime's endgame and strategy, or African Americans about the motives behind the infamous Jim Crow laws. But we Palestinians are cursed with the need to respond to this kind of question about the oppressor's grand motives behind torturing, occupying, and even killing us. We, after all, are the victims of Western Enlightenment![26]

Right from the beginning, Israel's policy towards Gaza has been genocidal, no matter whether this happens quickly (three massive wars on Gaza within a period of five years) or in slow motion (embodied in the imposed medieval blockade). Gaza is an

* Originally published in a slightly different form in Haidar Eid, "The Only Remaining Hope in Gaza Is Knowing This Nightmare Can Be Brought to an End," Opinion, *Mondoweiss*, November 20, 2019, mondoweiss.net. Reprinted with permission from the publisher.

open-air prison; two-thirds of its inmates are refugees entitled to their right of return in accordance with UN Resolution 194. They are a constant reminder of the original sin committed in 1948. Israel wants to punish them for their resistance, for not being subservient subjects, and make them give up on their internationally guaranteed right of return.

The right of return is the theme of our grand narrative, one apartheid Israel feels the need to completely eradicate. Add to this the fact that the Gaza Strip has been the cradle of Palestinian resistance against Israel's multitiered system of oppression, namely occupation, colonization, and apartheid.

Forget about Benjamin Netanyahu's need to solve his domestic problems with his arch rival Benny Gantz and his intention to divert the attention of the Israeli public from charges of corruption and abuse of power raised against him. That was not the case in 2009, 2012, and 2014. This, in fact, is an unchanging policy toward native Palestinians, one that is not unlike any other settler colony.[27]

Once again, we Palestinians have to be clear about what we want. As many of us have argued, we have given up on the official bodies of the international community to condemn these heinous crimes and act to put an end to them within the foreseeable future. Instead, we count on civil society organizations and freedom-loving people to act in any possible way to put pressure on their governments to end diplomatic ties with apartheid Israel and institute sanctions against it for all these war crimes and crimes against humanity.

Is it an exaggeration to say that we are extremely appalled by the complicit silence of the international community, including the Arab and Islamic world? The international community by and large for generations has failed the Palestinian people. This is why we, Palestinian civil society, prefer to ask international civil society organizations to take whatever step, however small, to show their support for Palestine and rejection of Israeli genocidal war crimes and crimes against humanity by demanding that their governments sanction the only remaining apartheid state until it complies with international law. It worked against the inhumane apartheid regime in the second half of last century and ultimately led to its demise in 1994, with the election of Nelson Mandela as the first

African president of multiracial South Africa, and the creation of a new secular democratic state for all of its citizens regardless of race, gender, and ethnicity.

This is the only remaining hope we are nurturing these days, knowing very well that the nightmare can be brought to an end.

June 20, 2020

WHAT NEEDS TO BE DONE

The Israeli government, headed by Benjamin Netanyahu, is intent on annexing at least 30 percent of the occupied West Bank.* By doing this, the Zionist movement, which has historically denied the national and cultural rights of the indigenous population of Palestine, will finally kill the racist two-state solution, paving the way for an extended form of institutionalized and militarized apartheid that includes both the 1948 and 1967 areas.

Israel has always been clear that its objective is to occupy the entire land of "Israel"; that is, historic Palestine in addition to the Syrian Golan Heights. But where does that leave the Palestinian people? In South Africa, the apartheid regime decided to keep part of the Black African population in Bantustans, while others were left to rot in townships. If only those natives had accepted their fate as inferior creatures, things would have remained the same! But that was not the choice of the Africans and those who believed in equality. There was no compromise whatsoever on this basic human right. By contrast, in Palestine, we decided to start marathon negotiations with the Israelis in the hope that we would be granted an "independent homeland" for only one-third of us, forgetting the rights of the other two-thirds of the Palestinian people, namely refugees and Palestinian citizens of Israel.

The late Israeli prime minister Yitzhak Shamir was hoping to drag on negotiations with the representatives of the 1967 Palestinians from the West Bank and Gaza Strip for ten years. The negotiations lasted for more than two decades, leading to a de facto situation where it has become impossible for the Palestinians to have their own "independent" state on less than 22 percent of historic Palestine.

* Originally published in a slightly different form in Haidar Eid, "What Needs to Be Done," One Democratic State Campaign, June 20, 2020, onestatecampaign.org. Reprinted with permission from the publisher.

It is said that the late Palestinian leader Yasser Arafat realized in 2000, at the Camp David summit, that he was getting nothing from Israel and that he was expected to give up Jerusalem and the right of return of six million refugees. In exchange he would be granted tiny pieces of land, disconnected from each other, that he would be allowed to call "Palestine." And that is what the government of Israel and its American backers described as a "generous offer!"

In the meantime, Israel never stopped creating facts on the ground by expropriating more and more land, annexing it to the existing Israeli colonies, building a monstrous apartheid wall, kicking Jerusalemites out of their homes, and caging two million Palestinians in the tiny ghetto of Gaza. In fact, what was being created on the ground is a one-state reality that no Israeli or Palestinian leader wanted to recognize.

Looking at this history, it is clear what the goal of the Israeli colonizers has been from the start: the establishment of apartheid and the liquidation of the Palestinian cause all together. Full stop.

So, given this—what is to be done?

This is a question for the colonized Palestinians to address following the catastrophic failure of their choice to negotiate for three decades despite the huge power imbalance with the Israelis, out of the belief that the Americans and the spineless European Union would exert some sort of pressure on Israel to grant them an "independent" state. This possibility has now evaporated, with the right-wing Israeli government not mincing its words or intentions: one Jewish state between the Jordan River and the Mediterranean Sea.

First of all, we must admit that we have failed miserably to liberate even one inch of historic Palestine since 1948.

The emergence of our contemporary revolution in 1965, and the formation of the PLO one year before that were two important moments, among others, in the formation of a national identity that is denied by the Zionist colonizers. But now, we need to move forward. We can no longer afford to flirt with Zionism and reactionary Arab regimes. The threat is existential and, therefore, has to be dealt with in a manner that does not compromise on basic rights.

It is the right time to create the groundwork for a "new" political movement that will speak to a greater number of constituencies than traditional nationalist parties and progressive political organizations, who have surrendered to the seduction of assimilation by the Oslo "ideology," have proved capable of doing.

It's very encouraging to see more Palestinian activists embracing a clearer analysis that reflects a vision that is able to move beyond the racist two-state solution by radically critiquing the activism and nationalist theories of the past.

One good example is the formation of the One Democratic State Campaign, which has members from the three components of the Palestinian people. Its objective has been stated very clearly: replacing the apartheid regime with a democratic state of equal rights for all its inhabitants, including the returning refugees. Its vision is "a democracy that will give all the inhabitants of [Palestine] equal rights, will finally bring home the refugees, and will respect the cultures, religions, and identities of all the peoples that comprise our society."

This is precisely why it is of paramount importance that we situate the one-state discourse, and BDS, within the Palestinian radical tradition through links to the works of Ghassan Kanafani, Edward Said, and the anti-Stalinist Left.

We in Palestine do need a movement that pays attention to popular political education and moves away from the hegemonic, factional dichotomy. This movement has to prioritize work and activism on the ground, what South African activists referred to as "mass mobilization," and link that to the global BDS campaign that has already acknowledged the intersectionality of many current issues.

Gaza 2021

WEDHA STREET MASSACRE

May 16, 2021

ISRAEL'S WEHDA STREET MASSACRE SHOWS IT SEEKS TO ANNIHILATE US. WE WON'T LET IT

I am writing this while civil defence fighters are still retrieving bodies from beneath the rubble of the buildings that were brought down on their residents' heads on Al Wehda Street in Rimal, one of the most crowded, and affluent, neighbourhoods of Gaza City.* So far, 34 bodies have been recovered, all of whom are civilians, including children and women. This has brought the death toll since apartheid Israel has started its massive onslaught on Gaza four days ago to 188, including 55 children, 33 women, and 1,230 injuries.

Every time apartheid Israel commits a horrendous massacre in Palestine, in general, and in Gaza, in particular, some liberal Western journalists try to make us explain why it, the colonial power, is doing this. And "how do we respond" to its claims that it is "us" who are to blame? Mind you, these mostly white journalists never tried to ask Nelson Mandela what he had to say about apartheid South Africa's outrageous lies that he was a terrorist. Or Martin Luther King Jr. why he was accused of being an "agent provocateur!" In fact, the reason we get this question is a combination of racism, Islamophobia, and Orientalism. And this is partly how apartheid Israel gets away with its crimes against humanity and war crimes.

Israel is an apartheid, settler-colonial entity that, not unlike other settler colonies, denies the humanity of the native. It is one that is ideologically based on the "annihilation" of the "savage" Arab, whether in 1948 or seventy-three years later. It is not a

* Originally published in a slightly different form in Haidar Eid, "Israel's Wehda Street Massacre Shows It Seeks to Annihilate Us. We Won't Let It," Opinion, *Mondoweiss*, May 16, 2021, mondoweiss.net. Reprinted with permission from the publisher.

coincidence, then, that it decided to remind us of its original sin, namely, the Nakba, by celebrating its "independence" in Sheikh Jarrah and Gaza. By committing the Wehda Street massacre, it has taken the so-called conflict to its origin, dealing a blow to the two-state solution, the Oslo Accords, and the "peace industry."

Three years ago, we, Palestinians of Gaza, decided to remind Israel and its Western backers of our existence by marching very peacefully on the eastern barbed wire surrounding the Gaza ghetto. More than three hundred of us were killed by Israeli Gestapo-like snipers stationed on the other side of the wire. Many more were maimed and injured. The American administration, at the time, decided to reward its ally by moving its embassy to Jerusalem after recognizing it as Israel's eternal capital. We do understand that our humanity does not register in official American, and Western, consciousness. We are simply the victims of their victims. We are expected to pay for all the pogroms committed by white Europeans against Jews! It is, alas, as simple as that. We are not lucky enough to have been born to Jewish mothers so as to get Israeli citizenship and become the spoiled kids of the mighty colonial powers of the world. No wonder, then, that President Joe Biden supports "Israel's right to defend itself"; but he didn't accept South African apartheid's "right" to defend itself against indigenous Africans.

I keep thinking about where we are heading, what with apartheid Israel's daily crimes against the sons, daughters, and grandchildren of the victims of its original sin. I don't belong to the Nakba generation, but my parents did. They both died in a refugee camp dreaming of returning, or at least of being buried in their village. That didn't happen. This is why I joined the Great March of Return. And every single time I joined the Great March of Return on the eastern barbed wire surrounding besieged Gaza and separating Palestine from Palestine, my shadow would leave me and cross the line to the other side. When it returned, it was sad and silent as if it was the shadow of another man, until one day it went and never came back.

Since that moment, I have been living without my shadow.

I am here, it is there!

And this is why Israel committed the Wehda Street massacre, trying to annihilate us, together with our shadows on the other side of the barbed wire.

We will bury our martyrs, sing songs of freedom for them, and promise to bring the shadow back to the body. This is the least we can do for the memory of those killed last night.

May 27, 2021

AN APARTHEID DÉJÀ VU

In 2019, I wrote a piece for Al Jazeera, in which I reiterated that we, Palestinians of Gaza, have already made our choice.* I wrote: "We will not die a slow and dishonourable death while thanking our killers and labouring under the self-deception that portrays slavery to the occupier as a fait accompli." Our struggle is nonsectarian, one that is enshrined in the basic principles of the International Declaration on Human Rights, no matter how hard the hypocritical Western media tries to conceal the truth.

And now apartheid Israel has decided to launch yet another murderous campaign of bombardment against one of the most densely populated areas on earth, the Gaza Strip. Again, the victims include innocent civilians: children, women, and men. Some two hundred Palestinians have been killed, including forty children. On May 15, dozens of Palestinians were massacred in Al Wehda Street in downtown Gaza City alone.

Medical staff have also not been spared. On May 16, Dr. Ayman Abu Alouf, head of the internal medicine department of the Al-Shifa Medical Complex, was killed along with most of his family.

With American-made F-16 fighter jets, Israel has bombed and flattened dozens of residential buildings and hundreds of homes.

Ambulance and civil defence crews have been attempting for days now to retrieve Palestinians who have been buried by rubble, some using their mobile phones to call for help before taking their last breaths.

The message is very clear to us—it is civilians that Israel is after!

Once again, apartheid Israel has deployed its long-standing Dahiya doctrine—a blueprint for massacre and devastation

* Originally published in a slightly different form in Haidar Eid, "Gaza 2021: An Apartheid Déjà vu," Opinion, *Al-Jazeera*, May 17, 2021, aljazeera.com. Reprinted with permission from the publisher.

outlined by Gadi Eisenkot, head of the army's northern division, after the 2006 Israeli war on Lebanon.

Having decimated the Dahiya neighbourhood of Beirut with a vicious thirty-four-day air bombardment, Eisenkot declared, "What happened in the Dahiya quarter of Beirut in 2006 will happen in every village from which Israel is fired on . . . From our standpoint, these are not civilian villages, they are military bases."

In other words, every resident of Gaza, even a day-old baby, is a legitimate military target for Israel.

The ultimate goal of the Israelis is to brutalize Palestinians into submission, into giving up any resistance, any claim to their own land. As former Defence Minister Moshe Yaalon said in 2002, for the Israeli army, victory would be "sear[ing] into the Palestinian and Arab consciousness" that "terrorism and violence (read: resistance) will not defeat us."

As with previous massacres, this time once again Israel and the Palestinians—the oppressor and the oppressed—are equated as "two sides to a conflict" and what constitutes legitimate resistance under international law is put on the same level as a brutal illegal occupation. US President Joe Biden says apartheid Israel has the right to defend itself. The fact that Israel has an actual army, disproportionately greater firepower, and is an occupier is neglected as usual, as is the stark difference in the death toll. Biden, Boris Johnson, Angela Merkel, and other Western leaders and their "house Arabs" are just incapable of seeing the humanity of Palestinians.

Despite all the evidence, they refuse to recognize that this is an occupation, launched by a settler-colonial power that seeks to ethnically cleanse an entire indigenous population in order to solidify and legitimize its colony. What is happening in Gaza is incremental genocide, not a "security operation." And yet Palestinians are being asked to give in to a slow death, die aimlessly, showing no form of rebellion, and accept that if they die resisting, then it would be their own fault.

The question on Palestinian minds is: Why is this allowed to happen, twenty-seven years after the fall of the apartheid regime of South Africa? We know why Israel is doing it—we are the unwanted goyim, the refugees whose very existence is a constant reminder of the original sin committed in 1948, the premeditated crime of ethnic cleansing of the Palestinian people.

In Gaza, we know that Israel is going to get away with it, simply because it has never been held to account for any of the massacres it has committed. We also know that it is going to commit more and worse crimes. The United Nations, the European Union, the Arab League, the so-called international community at large, have failed the Palestinian people and will continue to do so.

The question is: What more do people who love freedom need to see in terms of death and destruction to translate their words of support into action? What more than the dead bodies of hundreds of Palestinian children? No child, whether Jewish, Hindu, Muslim, Christian, or of any other religion should see what Palestinian children are seeing right now.

Palestinians will no longer accept the dictates of the so-called international community that continues to favour Israel and cover up its war crimes. In light of the great sacrifices made by our people, any talk of merely improving the conditions of our oppression is a betrayal of the Palestinian victims of Israeli war crimes.

We do not want crumbs. We want to return to our lands and we want to live in them with our full rights under international law.

It is the ethical responsibility of every single person who believes in freedom for all to make sure that genocide and apartheid do not happen again.

This is why we say now that boycott, divestment, and sanctions against Israel is the responsibility not only of civil society organizations, but of every single individual. This is what we can all do. We can boycott Israeli goods and Israeli institutions, divest from Israeli businesses and demand sanctions on the Israeli government.

If we do so together and in solidarity, only then will Israel start to reconsider what it has done to the Palestinians.

Gaza could be the spark that initiates a different Palestine between the Jordan River and Mediterranean in the heart of the Middle East. The current uprising in the West Bank and Palestinian towns in Israel could be the birth pangs of a new reality characterized by the end of the racist two-state solution and the establishment of a secular democratic state on the historic land of Palestine, an inclusive state like South Africa.

Let the Gaza war in 2009 be like South Africa's 1960 Sharpeville massacre, in which white apartheid police opened fire on unarmed Black protestors, triggering a movement that brought down apartheid. Let the 2021 massacre in Gaza be the beginning of a new, more democratic Middle East, with a secular, democratic state of Palestine that treats all its citizens equally, regardless of religion, race, and gender.

December 10, 2021

THE CONSTRUCTION OF ISRAEL'S GAZA CONCENTRATION CAMP IS COMPLETE

Merriam-Webster dictionary defines a concentration camp as "a place where large numbers of people (such as prisoners of war, political prisoners, refugees, or the members of an ethnic or religious minority) are detained or confined under armed guard —used especially in reference to camps created by the Nazis in World War II for the internment and persecution of Jews and other prisoners."* And a death camp is "a concentration camp in which large numbers of prisoners are systematically killed."

The Gaza Strip, occupied and besieged by apartheid Israel, has been transformed into both; the difference is that it is larger than all known concentration and death camps created by the bigoted Western regimes in the twentieth century. Israel's decision to redeploy its troops around the densely populated coastal strip in 2005, and then impose an unprecedented, medieval siege in 2006 that has shattered all spheres of life, and then carry out four massive attacks that have killed more than four thousand civilians, including women and children, does not seem to be enough for the ruling Zionist elites of the rogue state.

Two days ago, it announced the completion of a sensor-equipped underground wall around Gaza that includes hundreds of cameras, radar, and other sensors, and spans sixty-five kilometres. It was reported that the wall is more than six metres high and its maritime barrier includes electronic devices to detect infiltration by sea and a remote-controlled weapons system. The

* Originally published in a slightly different form in Haidar Eid, "The Construction of Israel's Gaza Concentration Camp Is Complete," Opinion, *Mondoweiss*, December 10, 2021, mondoweiss.net. Reprinted with permission from the publisher.

ministry did not disclose the depth of the underground wall. It took three and a half years to complete.

Not a single mainstream media outlet used the term "concentration camp," or even apartheid, in reference to the ongoing siege of the Gaza Strip. The language used by the IOF has become the reference—no questions asked. No Gazan/Palestinian voice is permitted to say a word about the impact of this "project" on their lives. What we get to read is the statement made by Israeli war criminal, Defence Minister Benny Gantz, "The barrier, which is an innovative and technologically advanced project, deprives Hamas of one of the capabilities it tried to develop," and that "[it] places an 'iron wall,' sensors and concrete between the terror organization and the residents of Israel's south." *Period!* No questions asked!

The two million residents of the Gaza Strip have to be imprisoned inside this concentration camp because they are all "Hamas supporters," and that gives "us" the right to use a "smart wall" to encircle "them." That is not a form of "collective punishment" only because "they" are not born to Jewish mothers, and, therefore, they do not have the "right" to be treated as full human beings. Only those with white skin and/or born to Jewish families can have that right.

These are the same systems of oppression that were used in apartheid South Africa and the American South under Jim Crow; they have become all too familiar in Palestine.

And now we have to deal with the fact that we are literally inmates of the largest concentration camp on earth with no rights whatsoever. President Carter was not exaggerating when he said, after visiting Gaza in 2009, "[Palestinians in the Gaza Strip] are being treated more like animals than human beings . . . Never before in history has a large community like this been savaged by bombs and missiles and then been deprived of the means to repair itself."

Alas, Carter is no longer president of the US, the strategic ally of apartheid Israel. As long as world official bodies and leaders choose to say and do absolutely nothing, Israel will go on killing more Palestinians, building higher walls, tightening the siege, and claiming it is all done in "self-defence!"

And yet we, ungrateful "antisemites," are blamed for calling it a "concentration camp!"

November 21, 2022

REFLECTIONS FROM GAZA AFTER ISRAEL'S ELECTIONS

When my refugee students ask me about the meaning of "Orientalism," I tell them to look at Israel.* Prejudice, fantasies, and racist clichés purveyed by Zionism about Palestinians and Arabs and colonial abuse of power and domination by one self-proclaimed superior culture over another.

Like the inhumane apartheid system before it, apartheid Israel is unable to understand Palestinian suffering and the nature of its oppression of those living in Gaza. This is part of what the late Edward Said calls "blaming the victim."[28]

Nothing whatsoever justifies the theft of other people's lands and intimate memories. This is a crime against humanity; it is immoral and unethical. This is why settler colonialism in Palestine should be condemned. It is time for the international community to declare all those organizations that support settlements and settler colonialism in Palestine illegal.

In his groundbreaking *Politics of Dispossession*, reiterating Ghassan Kanafani's argument in *Returning to Haifa*, Edward Said states very convincingly:

> The question to be asked is how long can the history of anti-Semitism and the Holocaust in particular be used as a fence to exempt Israel from arguments and sanctions against it for its behaviour toward the Palestinians, arguments and sanctions that were used against other repressive governments, such as that of South Africa. How long are we going to deny that the

* Originally published in a slightly different form in Haidar Eid, "Reflections from Gaza After Israel's Elections," *Palestine Chronicle*, November 21, 2021, palestinechronicle.com. Reprinted with permission from the publisher.

> cries of the people of Gaza are directly connected to the policies of the Israeli government and not to the cries of the victims of Nazism?[29]

It is indicative of the official Israeli mindset that the genocidal siege of the Gaza Strip never seemed to register in the Jewish state's overall strategy. And now we have Benjamin Netanyahu making a triumphant return with his fascist allies, Ben-Gvir and Bezalel Smotrich. As far as Israelis or Israeli officials are concerned, Israel withdrew its troops and settlers from Gaza in 2005, leaving Gaza free.

However, it has kept the keys to the crossings separating it from Gaza and has left the last crossing in the hands of its Egyptian allies. As far as Israeli mainstream politicians are concerned, the Palestinians of Gaza are very ungrateful for not accepting the blockade, for resisting it, and for demanding their internationally sanctioned rights!

In fact, supported by an international conspiracy of silence, not to say collusion, Israel's aim is to make us become so habituated to oppression that we cease to feel it as oppression. As simple as that. The so-called international community has decided to remain deaf despite the glaring fact of clause 50 of the 1907 Hague Convention stating unequivocally the international community's rejection of collective punishment. This was reiterated by the Fourth Geneva Convention in Clause 33 of 1949. As Ajamu Baraka pointed out on his Facebook page during the first days of the Russian attack on Ukraine:

> I embrace "whataboutism" because so-called "whataboutism" is nothing more than critical dialectical thinking that informs the struggle against bourgeois ideological mystification. The ideological responsibility of revolutionary socialists is to reveal what is hidden, denounce what is being silenced and recontextualize the attempts to de-contextualize issues, ideas and practices.

As if Israel's blockade of Gaza is not enough, it seems that Palestine's class character revealed itself in resentment towards the

Palestinians of Gaza who are perceived as Hamas supporters and members and therefore constitute a serious threat to the so-called national project.

As a result, one of the most repeated (Western) questions that we have to deal with is: But what does "lifting the siege" mean?

It basically means the opening of the six crossings, the keys to which are in Israel's hands, and the flow of all kinds of goods, especially essentials, to and from Gaza. It means providing Gaza with electricity and clean water and guaranteeing the freedom of movement of the two million Palestinians of Gaza. It also means the permanent opening of the Rafah crossing.

This is the responsibility of the occupying power, namely Israel. But even this does not meet the minimum basic rights of the Palestinian people, namely freedom, equality, and justice. No normal relations with apartheid Israel should be resumed without the latter complying with international law that guarantees Palestinian basic rights.

One day, like in South Africa, we will have victim impact statements whereby we tell our killers from Benjamin Netanyahu to Gantz to Yair Lipid how they have forever turned our lives upside down.

Gaza 2023

GENOCIDE

October 10, 2023

OUR WARSAW UPRISING MOMENT

It is Gaza again![*] But it is different this time! Instead of reacting to one of apartheid Israel's regular genocidal attacks, the resistance movements have taken the "first" step in an unprecedented move.

Instead of waiting for Israel's "generosity" when it decides, through mediators, to open one of the seven gates of the largest open-air prisons on earth, the inmates—having learned from the Warsaw Uprising of 1944—decided to bring it down themselves.

The deadly medieval siege that has been imposed on Gaza since 2007—supported by the European Union and the United States—along with recurrent genocidal wars launched by Israel are an attempt to make the Palestinians of Gaza disappear—albeit slowly and painfully.

No more! Enough is enough.

The resistance movements in Gaza, Right and Left, have decided to turn the table upside down. They have given the Palestinian struggle a new impetus, a clear direction towards liberation and decolonization.

A Truncated Palestinian History

To understand the events of today, it is important to remember the context of the Palestinian struggle of the past thirty years. The decision by the leadership of the Palestinian Liberation Organization to do what used to be unthinkable—coexist with Zionism—led to the disastrous Oslo Accords, which, in effect, truncated Palestinian history.

The Naksa—the Israeli occupation of the West Bank, Gaza, the Golan Heights, and the Sinai desert in 1967 became separate

* Originally published in a slightly different form in Haidar Eid, "Gaza 2023: Our Warsaw Uprising Moment," Opinion, *Al-Jazeera*, October 10, 2023, aljazeera.com. Reprinted with permission from the publisher.

from the Nakba—the mass expulsion of Palestinians from their homeland in 1948.

The focus became the occupation and not the settler colonialism that stood behind it, while "peace negotiations" served as a cover for Israeli violence and the continued dispossession of the Palestinians.

As Israeli historian Ilan Pappé maintains in his book *The Biggest Prison on Earth*:

> Israeli strategists discovered that if you want to implement ethnic cleansing by other means, the alternative to expulsion is not to allow people to leave the place where they live—and thus they can be excluded from the democratic balance of power. They are contained inside their own areas, but do not have to be counted in the overall national demographics since they cannot freely move, develop or expand, nor do they have any basic civil and human rights.

Apartheid Israel has made it absolutely clear that since it cannot get rid of us completely, we must become its slaves, people without any rights.

The majority of Israeli Jews support the genocidal policy of their governments because, as Zionists living in apartheid Israel, they are indoctrinated into believing that they are entitled to certain privileges that must be denied to the indigenous population of the land.

In 1948, to implement this racist ideology, ethnic cleansing was the solution. And in 1967, enslavement became the only option.

In the face of this reality, Palestinians have reached common ground on the enemy being settler colonialism, but they have failed to agree on how decolonization should be understood and achieved.

In recent years, there has been a radical shift in the strategic thinking on this point, one that looks at Israeli-Palestinian relations within the framework of settler colonialism and apartheid.

True liberation within this context means achieving true equality in historic Palestine after the return of all Palestinian refugees to the towns and villages from which they were ethnically cleansed in 1948.

A Vision of Liberation

No wonder Gaza has decided to take this unprecedented move. Two-thirds of Gazans are refugees entitled to their right of return in accordance with United Nations General Assembly (UNGA) Resolution 194 of 1948.

It is rumoured that the resistance fighters who managed to enter Sderot are the grandsons of refugees from the village of Huj, which was ethnically cleansed by Zionist militias in 1948 and renamed Sderot. Others are from the village of Hirbya, renamed Zikim by the Israelis.

They have dared to do the "unthinkable"; that is, return, not as visitors granted permission by the colonizer, but as liberators upholding their right to their ancestral land.

This radical act of return points to the post-Zionist future we should envision that will bring liberation to all.

Liberation for us means dismantling the structures of Zionist settler colonialism and apartheid and addressing the inequalities and injustices it has inflicted on us, the indigenous population of Palestine, over the past hundred years.

Liberation for us aims to transform the relationship between Palestinians and Israelis into one based on total equality and justice. The settler society is expected to abandon all colonial privileges and display real willingness to accept responsibility for past crimes and injustices. The compromise that indigenous Palestinians are expected to offer is to accept settlers as equal citizens in the new state between the Jordan River and the Mediterranean Sea.

This is the path to peace and security, and the international community, which has long accepted Israel's war crimes against the Palestinians and has even been complicit in them, will have to embrace it.

Having learned nothing from history, US President Joe Biden made it clear the day Palestinian fighters crossed through the barbed wire to Israel that he is fully behind Israel, giving its army the green light to commit more war crimes against the civilians of Gaza.

Three days after the start of the resistance inside 1948 Palestine, Israel has killed more than 770 people in Gaza, including 140 children, and injured 4,000. More than 180,000 people have had to flee their homes as their neighbourhoods have been viciously targeted by Israeli war planes; I am one of them.

Leaders like Biden would do well to remember Brazilian educator and philosopher Paulo Freire's words:

> With the establishment of a relationship of oppression, violence has already begun. Never in history has violence been initiated by the oppressed. How could they be the initiators, if they themselves are the result of violence? . . . There would be no oppressed had there been no prior situation of violence to establish their subjugation. Violence is initiated by those who oppress, who exploit, who fail to recognize others as people—not by those who are oppressed, exploited, and unrecognized.[30]

In Gaza and Jenin, we refuse to march to Israel's death chambers like sheep. In Gaza and Jenin—in fact, in all of historic Palestine—we have made it absolutely clear that we will resist the settler, colonial, apartheid regime between the Jordan River and the Mediterranean.

And we expect the international community to support our struggle for justice and freedom in exactly the same way as it has supported the Ukrainian resistance against the Russian invasion.

The double standards we have seen have convinced us that it is our duty as Palestinians to create the political space for our liberation where none has been afforded to us.

We cannot compromise on our basic rights, including the right to self-determination and the right of return. We have a clear path towards liberation that strays away from the façade of talking independence and camouflaged racist solutions.

October 15, 2023

FROM GAZA WE ASK YOU TO STAND UP AGAINST GENOCIDE!

> What happens in Gaza is the defining moment of our time, which either grants the impunity of war criminals the immunity of our silence, while we contort our own intellect and morality, or gives us the power to speak out.
>
> —John Pilger, *Newstatesman*

The Israeli war crimes committed against our people in the Gaza Strip are unprecedented, a combination of ethnic cleansing and genocide.*

Ordinary people in Gaza expect the international community and the Arab and Islamic worlds to take up their responsibility to protect the Palestinian people from these heinous crimes and immediately terminate Israel's unfolding genocide.

Nothing whatsoever justifies the Israeli savagery, including the severing of the water and electricity supply to 2.3 million people, half of them children.

No medical supplies are coming in either. Children, the sick, and the elderly are the first to be affected.

Since Saturday, October 7, Israel has flattened entire neighbourhoods, including mine, al-Rimal.

It has destroyed vital bridges, roads, water and electricity stations, residential towers, and villas, on top of their occupants. Dozens of entire families have been wiped out.

Among the latest victims is Professor Omar Firwana, the dean of the medical faculty at the Islamic University of Gaza. He was wiped out along with his entire family.

* Originally published in a slightly different form in Haidar Eid, "From Gaza We Ask You to Stand Up Against Genocide!" *Electronic Intifada*, October 15, 2023, electronicintifada.net. Reprinted with permission from the publisher.

No Food, No Water

The latest from the Ministry of Health is that more than 2,300 of us have been killed by the nonstop Israeli bombardments, including more than 700 children—an extermination rate that averages 100 children per day.

The toll of injured is over 9,000, but the reality is that the numbers are likely much higher as poorly equipped rescue teams cannot possibly reach all those under the countless destroyed buildings and massacre sites.

By Saturday, about 600,000 people had been evacuated from northern Gaza and Gaza City to the south.

Three hospitals, including al-Shifa, Gaza's largest, were ordered by Israel to evacuate, but they are refusing to do that. Transporting the sick and injured is simply impossible, with constant bombardment, little fuel, and no safe facilities to which they can be transferred. And every hour hundreds more injured are coming in. They cannot simply be abandoned to their fate.

UN officials are now warning that the hospitals in Gaza could cease functioning altogether within forty-eight hours, as fuel for emergency generators is about to run out.

Food, as scarce as it is now, cannot be preserved as there is no electricity.

People are already experiencing severe dehydration due to lack of water.

There is an increasing threat of the spread of disease because of lack of water.

Conspiracy of Silence

The Palestinian people in Gaza had already been under siege for the past seventeen years as collective punishment for exercising their democratic choice in elections in January 2006.

Since then, Israel has turned the Gaza Strip into the largest concentration camp with the largest population of prisoners in the world, and called it "withdrawal."

The international conspiracy of silence towards the genocidal war taking place against the 2.3 million civilians in Gaza indicates complicity in these war crimes.

In fact, Western governments, especially the United States, are directly involved in these war crimes and crimes against humanity, as evidenced by the statements in total support of Israel's crimes made by the highest-ranking officials including President Joe Biden, Secretary of State Antony Blinken, and Defence Secretary Lloyd Austin.

We Make These Demands!

Here from Gaza, we demand that:

- the rogue state of Israel end its genocidal attacks; and
- the UN send troops to protect us civilians, after the immediate entry of humanitarian aid.

As for Palestine solidarity groups and all international civil society organizations, we expect them to demand:

- the immediate end of the unfolding genocide;
- the protection of civilian lives and property, as stipulated in international humanitarian law and international human rights law, including the Fourth Geneva Convention;
- that Palestinian refugees in the Gaza Strip be provided with financial and material support to cope with the immense hardship that they are experiencing; and
- immediate reparations and compensation for all the destruction carried out by IOF in the Gaza Strip, including psychological counselling for the collective mental trauma of Palestinian civilians.

It's Time to Stand Up

We are aware that the colonial West has historically accepted Israel trampling all over Palestinians, from the beginning in 1948.

With precision brutality we have been uprooted, humiliated at checkpoints, imprisoned without charge, denied our heritage and religious sites, denied our freedom to move and see family members, denied water and our livelihoods, our arable land, our access to the sea, our dreams of visiting other countries.

And Israel has carried on because it knows the West makes noises but it does not stand up to it.

Europe and the US have not merely watched from the sidelines, they have actively assisted Israel and rewarded it for its crimes, even this genocide.

Indeed, the colonial West has decided to get directly involved while fully reviving orientalist, racist stereotypes about barbaric brown Arabs or, in the words of Yoav Gallant, Israel's minister of war, "human animals."

Hence the ease with which apartheid Israel has managed to mobilize mainstream media to endorse its racist narrative and cheer for its unspeakable crimes and massacres.

It is time to stand up!

Stand up for basic human rights! Is it too much to ask the world to follow basic expectations of human rights in its dealings with Israel?

Stand up against its policies of occupation, colonization, apartheid, and genocide!

When justice eventually comes and we can live as equals, not under apartheid and denied our rights and homes, people will look back aghast that such collective punishment, persecution, cruelty, and extermination was allowed to go on for so long, aided and abetted by the colonial West.

October 30, 2023

"DEMISE OF OFFICIAL ARAB SOLIDARITY WITH PALESTINE"

Arab regimes have given up on the idea of liberating Palestine.*

Gamal Abdel Nasser, the progressive, nationalist president of Egypt, was the last Arab leader to really believe in and work on the idea. For him, liberating Palestine was a core issue that could not be separated from Egypt's national security.

He made it absolutely clear that the establishment of Israel in the heart of the Arab world was a huge blow to Arab aspirations for modernity, progress, prosperity, and freedom. It embodied the continuation of colonialism in a postcolonial Arab world.

A settler colony had been founded that negated the very existence of the Palestinian people and, hence, posed a threat to Egypt and the rest of the Arab world.

That is, perhaps, the main reason why Nasser's progressive regime, with its anti-colonial leanings, was targeted by ex-colonial powers, namely Britain and France, both of which got directly involved in an alliance with Israel to topple Nasser's government in 1956, and by America, which formed its own alliance with Israel in 1967.

The demise of Nasser in 1970 was a turning point. His successor, Anwar Sadat, followed a completely different line in terms of relations with the Western world and Israel.

Sadat strongly believed that 99 percent of the cards were in America's hands, as he scandalously put it. The US was the only power, he believed, that could persuade Israel to grant the concessions needed to return occupied Egyptian lands in the Sinai and even "solve" the Palestinian question.

* Originally published in a slightly different form in Haidar Eid, "Gaza Genocide Enabled by Arab Leaders," *Electronic Intifada*, October 30, 2023, electronicintifada.net. Reprinted with permission from the publisher.

That was part and parcel of a new domestic—albeit reactionary—"open door" economic policy of privatization and restructuring the public sector. Gone were the official commitments to pan-Arabism and the liberation of Palestine.

Freedom Seen as an Obstacle

Normalization with apartheid Israel became the "solution" on the basis of offering the Palestinians a form of "autonomy" in the West Bank and the Gaza Strip: land in exchange for "peace" and recognizing Israel's right to exist as a settler colony in the heart of the Arab world. That was the motive behind the signing of the Camp David Accords (1978) and the beginning of a series of normalization accords between Arab governments, including the PLO and Israel.

Arab governments willing to "normalize" relations with Israel have always considered the Palestinian cause as an obstacle to their own "prosperity and security." An obstacle to be moved out of the way.

Liberating Palestine was no longer on the agenda. It was deemed an unrealistic dream that cannot be achieved no matter what.

Supporting a just solution to the Palestinian question necessarily means a confrontation with the imperialist West, headed by the United States. And that is a route Arab regimes are not keen to follow.

First, it goes against the interests of the ruling oligarchies.

Second, it weakens their alliance with the US, a superpower that offers them protection and stability.

Hence the demise of the ideas of liberating Palestine and the return of Palestinian refugees to the towns and villages from which they were ethnically cleansed back in 1948. That has been replaced by the facade of the racist, two-state solution and the idea that it is possible to improve apartheid Israel and its multitiered system of oppression of the Palestinian people.

Shameful Silence

Even the very definition of the Palestinian people itself has been reduced to include only those who currently live in the Gaza Strip and the West Bank. This group is said to be the component of the

Palestinian people that needs a "solution," and that solution can only materialize if apartheid Israel generously offers to improve the lives of these Palestinians, even if this happens under Israel's total control.

A "generous offer" from Israel might include what Amilcar Cabral—one of Africa's most prominent opponents of colonialism—called "flag independence," symbols of governance and "sovereignty." Hence official Arab support for the Oslo Accords in 1993, which offered a fig leaf to all subsequent Arab deals of normalization with apartheid Israel.

For more than three weeks now, Israel has been attacking Gaza, killing thousands and injuring tens of thousands, destroying most of the infrastructure and sending it back to the "stone age."

Would Israel have the "courage" to do so without the shameful silence of Arab governments? Or to put it more crudely, would this have happened had the normalization deals not been signed?

After more than three weeks of unfolding genocide, there doesn't seem to be an end in sight. This bloody mayhem is redolent of World War II and the times of genocidal pogroms in Eastern Europe, Africa, Australia, and the Americas.

Gaza is literally being wiped out.

The Palestinians of Gaza, both Muslims and Christians, are Arabs whose humanity has been denied even by their "official" brethren. Otherwise, Israel's ethnic cleansing and genocide would not have been allowed to happen, even in the worst nightmares of the Arab states.

In 1956, Gamal Abdel Nasser paid a visit to Gaza and addressed its "heroic" people:

> People of Gaza, I want three things from you: Hope, patience and faith (in your cause). These three qualities will lead you to victory over all those powers conspiring against you. You are the noblest and most honourable people and I want you to know one important fact: Gaza is as dear to my heart as Egypt, and whatever harms Gaza harms Egypt.

That was a time when liberating Palestine was an achievable, realistic idea.

November 27, 2023

A CEASEFIRE IN A TIME OF GENOCIDE

The bitter reality for us, Palestinians in Gaza, is that we are alone, beleaguered, under siege, and seen as undesirables even by some of those who are supposed to be our brethren.* Forty-five days of barbaric massacres have claimed the lives of more than 14,000 people, including more than 6,000 children and 3,500 women.

Among the thousands of men who have been killed are university students, doctors, nurses, shop owners, and youth who were sent out by their families to search for food or water.

More than 7,000 are still missing, including 4,000 children—most of them are dead, buried under the rubble of their homes.

More are dying in bombed-out hospitals rendered inoperative and in the few that are still working but cannot cope with the tens of thousands of wounded due to the lack of staff and medical supplies. Soon even more will be dying of disease, hunger, and the winter cold.

Israel's deliberate targeting of civilian homes has completely wiped out hundreds of families from the population register. Some 1.7 million people have been displaced.

For forty-five days, Palestinians have been left alone to face the onslaught of the world's fourth strongest army, which possesses two hundred nuclear weapons, hundreds of F-16 jets, attack helicopters, gunboats, battle tanks, and armoured vehicles and hundreds of thousands of soldiers and reservists.

As the humanitarian tragedy in Gaza has reached unimaginable levels, some Arab regimes have done nothing more than issue timid statements, denouncing and condemning. Nothing more.

* Originally published in a slightly different form in Haidar Eid, "A Ceasefire in a Time of Genocide," Opinion, *Al-Jazeera*, November 27, 2023, aljazeera.com. Reprinted with permission from the publisher.

In fact, Arab regimes have let down the Palestinians since 1948, and to this day, official Arab positions are a combination of cowardice and hypocrisy. They have failed to bring an end to the Israeli siege on Gaza for seventeen years now and are now failing to stop Israel's genocide.

We in Gaza are now wondering how the timid expressions of support coming out of the streets and capitals of the Arab nations can be turned into concrete action in the absence of democracy. We wonder whether the Arabs living under the rule of authoritarian, oligarchical regimes can change them in nonviolent ways.

We exhaust ourselves trying to figure out the possible means available to achieve democratic political change because with the genocide in Gaza and the apartheid regime in the rest of Palestine, we have not seen any practical translation for the solidarity shown by some Arab peoples with Palestine.

Desmond Tutu, the late South African anti-apartheid activist and Anglican bishop, once said, "If you are neutral in situations of injustice, you have chosen the side of the oppressor."

As I argued during Israel's brutal assaults on Gaza in 2009, 2012, and 2014, the United Nations, the European Union, and Arab states have not been neutral; they have remained largely silent about the atrocities the Israeli forces have committed. Since thousands of corpses of women and children have failed to convince them of the need to act, they have taken Israel's side.

This state of affairs put two choices before the Palestinians in Gaza: dying dishonourably while thanking our killers for a trickle of food and water or fighting for our dignity, for ourselves and the coming generations. It is now clear that after years of self-deception that portrayed slavery to the occupier as a fait accompli, we have chosen the second option.

But instead of recognizing our resistance as such and seeing it in the context of the decades-long Palestinian struggle for freedom from occupation and apartheid, the international community is instead reducing it to a "conflict" between two "equal" sides.

The ongoing truce and the longer-term ceasefire initiative reflect this attitude. They in no way take into account that Israel has two clear objectives in its war on Gaza: the slaughter of the largest possible number of Palestinians by targeting Palestinian civilians and the elimination of any possibility of resistance in order to maintain stability in this open-air concentration camp.

It appears that what the international community is requiring of Palestinians is to behave as "house slaves" and be grateful for the crumbs their white masters are letting them have. They are to appreciate the trickle of food and water that is allowed to sustain them barely alive and accept their slow death. They are to concede that if they die, it is their own fault.

But Palestinians in Gaza and beyond will not oblige.

Accordingly, any agreement that does not lead to the immediate lifting of the blockade, the reopening of the Rafah crossing and all the other crossings in a manner that allows the introduction of food, fuel, medicine, and all other needs—in conjunction with an agreement that ends the Israeli occupation and apartheid and upholds the Palestinian right of return—will not be acceptable to the people of Gaza.

The biggest source of concern for the Israeli "masters," their Western allies, and their Arab lackeys would be for us to raise the ceiling of our demands to that level; to demand that the conflict be put in the context of the multifaceted settler-colonial enterprise, the occupation, the apartheid, and the ethnic cleansing.

October 7 is a pivotal moment in Palestinian history. Gaza and the rest of Palestine yearns for a leadership that rises up to the level of this historic moment, a leadership that would take the following measures without any further delay:

- Enacting a full cessation of security coordination with Israel.
- Going to the ICC and suing Israeli political and military leaders for war crimes and crimes against humanity.
- Reviewing all agreements signed with Israel, particularly the Oslo Accords and related agreements.
- Declaring a clear position on any initiative that does not take into account the need for the immediate end of the siege, the reopening of all crossings, and the restoration of the full freedom of movement.

Any talk about improving the conditions of oppression in light of the great sacrifices of Gaza is a betrayal of the Palestinian martyrs. It is time to start discussing radical solutions away from the "interim program" and the Bantustan-like state and adopt a clear slogan: end the occupation, end the apartheid, and end settler colonialism. This is the only way the loss of thousands of lives in Gaza would not have been in vain.

December 3, 2023

LEAVING GAZA

I left Gaza with my family on Dec. 3, 2023 and travelled to South Africa via Egypt, arriving December 5. In January 2024, I gave a live interview describing the journey.

The last two months, I must admit, have been the worst two months of my life, and I think that every single Gazan can say the same thing.* As you've mentioned, I came to South Africa with my wife and my two little kids. The worst part of it was the reaction of the kids. I have a seven-year-old daughter and a six-year-old daughter. So far, I've been displaced four times—with them. The first time was at the beginning of the genocide. At the end of the first week (I live in the al-Rimal neighbourhood in a residential tower), I was contacted by an Israeli intelligence officer and he asked us to evacuate. At the time, we misunderstood because we thought that they wanted to bring down the residential tower itself. Luckily, we learn from our experiences, and because of what happened in previous massacres, we decided to put our passports and identity cards and the girls' birth certificates and our marriage certificate in a small bag next to the door of the flat, right from the first day of the massacre, of the genocide. When he called us (and he knew my name) he said, "We want you to leave and head to the north," and at that time, they were shelling the north, in fact, so they were asking us to leave to an area where we would be definitely killed. We stayed with our neighbours in the opposite building and that was the first time they used a new military strategy they called a fire belt, where they attack the area with air strikes, constant air strikes, for seven or eight hours. So we were about seven or eight families trapped in one small corridor until 6:00 in the morning, inhaling strange

* Originally published in a slightly different form in Haidar Eid, "Breaking News and Analysis on Day 103 of Gaza's Al-Aqsa Flood," interview with Nora Barrows-Friedman, *Electronic Intifada*, podcast, 2:21:28 (interview begins at 12:46), January 17, 2024, youtube.com. Reprinted with permission from the publisher.

gas and, of course because I used my hands to close my daughter's ears, I lost my hearing. Yeah, so that was the price because they didn't know how to do that and, you know, they are little kids.

So, the following day, in the morning, we moved. We found out that the whole neighbourhood was flattened down, the whole neighborhood of al-Rimal was flattened. Our flat was uninhabitable. We had absolutely nothing, and I left my car in the garage under the rubble. We moved to the north where I stayed with my brother for three nights and the same scenario was repeated again but this time they wanted the entire population of Gaza City and the northern part of Gaza—we are talking about 1.1 million people—to move within six or seven hours. So we packed all my family, my brother's family, we were about twelve people in a small car and I drove. We reached Khan Yunis and I tell you, the scene, it was a repeat of the Nakba. Hundreds of thousands of people on horses, donkeys, trucks, lorries, cars, people walking, holding toddlers. It was unbelievable. We never thought—we were so naive to believe that the Israelis wouldn't be able or rather wouldn't be allowed to cross the red line and to repeat the scenario of the Nakba again. Yes, we were naive . . . we agreed the world would not allow another genocide, the first genocide in the twenty-first century. Anyway, I was driving and my brother, he was sitting next to me with his daughter and his son and about ten people were sitting in the back, he had a minor heart attack. And the surprise is that we found out we were the only people on that road, so of course, I couldn't go back. I had to accelerate, I had to press very hard on the accelerator until we arrived. Luckily, I don't know how it happened, we were the only people on the road and we could hear the bombing, and everybody was panicking, and I was trying to help my brother. We arrived safely, luckily, and we stayed with my sister. And the first night we arrived, the Israelis shelled the house next to my sister's house, and that was the second worst night in my life because my kids were screaming and I couldn't do anything.

My experience is nothing, nothing, compared to the sufferings of the hundreds of thousands of Palestinians and Gazans. I've lost forty of my cousins, with their sons, daughters, nieces, direct cousins, first cousins . . . In 2014 we were talking about Israel aiming to wipe out entire families. When we said families at that time we meant nuclear families, and now when we say families, we are talking about extended families, we are talking about clans. So, it's not one family but the entire clan. So, so many clans were wiped out.

It's very traumatic and it has been a very traumatizing experience for myself, for my family, for my friends, for every single Gazan I know. I've been through all the massacres since 2008—2012, 2014, 2021, and the Great March of Return—and every single time, because I have dual citizenship, the South African Embassy would contact me and ask me whether I would want to leave and every single time I said no. Well, I didn't have kids at the time. Now, this time, I lost my house, I lost my name, we lost Gaza. We've lost Gaza, Gaza is gone.

December 9, 2023

WHY DOES AMERICA HATE US?

Is Genocide Joe any better than Donald Trump?*

Why did the American president give apartheid Israel carte blanche to carry out its unprecedented genocide against the Palestinians of Gaza?

Why did he continue to do so with the US veto at the UN Security Council on December 8?

Why don't Palestinians register on the radar of the White House and mainstream America?

In other words, why does white America hate us?

One very telling moment in this regard came on January 6, 2021, when a mob of white racists stormed the Capitol in Washington demanding a reversal of the outcome of the presidential election in which their president and role model Donald Trump had lost to the Democrat's candidate, Joe Biden.

Biden won the election claiming that he would introduce a more democratic, humane and—more importantly—inclusive vision.

Philip Weiss, senior editor and founder of the pro-Palestinian website *Mondoweiss*, wrote a hard-hitting article titled "America's Whiteness Crisis, and Zionism's," just a few hours after the mob of white bigots stormed the Capitol.[31]

Weiss wrote that it was no coincidence to see Israeli flags brandished at the Capitol Hill riot because "Israel's proudly stated principle of Jewish supremacy, higher Jewish rights to land and office, have long been a model for white supremacists."

He argued, eloquently, that there are glaring contradictions between Israel's state ideology, Zionism, and democratic ideals. The contradictions are evident in Israel's more than sixty racist

* Originally published in a slightly different form in Haidar Eid, "Biden's White Supremacy Gives Israel Carte Blanche to Commit Genocide," *Electronic Intifada*, December 9, 2023, electronicintifada.net. Reprinted with permission from the publisher.

Basic Laws, including the notorious nation-state law that defines Israel as the state of Jews only.

As per the definition of apartheid under the Rome Statute of the ICC, Israel's practices towards Palestinians amount to "an institutionalized regime of systematic oppression and domination."

Who Cares About the ICC?

But Trump supporters, like Israeli Zionists, do not give a damn about the ICC and its definitions, nor do they know what basic human rights mean, nor do they see the humanity of the Other—whether Black, Palestinian, or Hispanic.

Neither do Biden and his state and defence secretaries.

Coincidentally, a couple of days after the Capitol riot, *The Guardian* ran a piece by Hagai El-Ad, then executive director of B'Tselem, Israel's most liberal human rights organization, the title of which is very telling: "We Are Israel's Largest Human Rights Group—and We Are Calling This Apartheid."[32]

El-Ad was blunt about Israel's apartheid and racism based on the "the systematic promotion of the supremacy of one group of people [the Jewish people] over another [the Palestinians]," which, he concludes, is "deeply immoral and must end."

Soon after that, a number of mainstream human rights organizations, including Human Rights Watch, Amnesty International, and B'Tselem itself, issued reports labelling Israel's regime between the Jordan River and the Mediterranean Sea as apartheid.

Different from South African apartheid and American segregation laws, "Israel's definitions do not depend on skin colour." But that makes no material difference; what really matters, according to El-Ad, is "the supremacist reality which is the heart of the matter."

He did not mince his words: it is "Jewish supremacy."

In the case of Make America Great Again (MAGA), it is racial supremacy; in apartheid Israel, it is ethno-religious. Hence the love affair between the two.

The comparison between the apartheid regime of South Africa and the American South under the Jim Crow laws is unavoidable. Ideology has its own way, especially when it is hegemonic—a way that represents the interests of racial supremacists. The white people of apartheid South Africa defined the institutions of the country as democratic—albeit a white democracy; that is, by and for whites only.

The idea of defining the country as exclusively white and democratic at the same time was never accepted by the international community. But that is the model for Trump's supporters, the bigots who stormed the Capitol and who happened to be overwhelmingly white; that is what MAGA is all about.

Model Ethnic Supremacy

And that, alas, seems to be the driving force behind Genocide Joe's love affair with apartheid Israel. Biden's Middle East policy is not in any way different to that of Donald Trump in that they are both a denial of the very existence of the Palestinian people.

What Trump supporters basically want is a state similar to both Israel and white South Africa, a state where the exclusive right of white people to "self-determination" is guaranteed.

Ironically, the same far-right that admires Israel happens to hate Jews—slogans such as Camp Auschwitz and 6 Million Was Not Enough were spotted, next to the Israeli flag, on Capitol Hill on January 6.

To explain this "contradiction," Philip Weiss quotes Jewish Voice for Peace: "Many white supremacist groups both hate Jews and love Israel."

Depending on their specific ideology, they may admire Israel as a model ethnic supremacist state, share its Islamophobic and anti-Arab views, and/or want Jews to be corralled in their own state far away from the US.

MAGA supporters seem to long for the days of "clearly defined white power and privilege" that would ideally lead to specifying the nature of the US as the nation-state of the white people.

Under this idea, the United States becomes the national home of white people and fulfills its natural, cultural, religious and historical right to self-determination (something Joe Biden claims to be opposed to).

MAGA supporters would also dearly want the right to exercise national self-determination in the United States to be unique to the white people (also rejected by Biden).

Sound familiar? That would be America's nation-state law if those far-right fascists got their way.

But is Genocide Joe better?

"I don't believe you have to be a Jew to be a Zionist, and I am a Zionist," Biden reportedly told the Israeli war cabinet in October.

Biden is a self-proclaimed Zionist who is NOT opposed to Israel being the state of Jews only and its right to "defend itself" as an apartheid state.

Palestinians have obviously joined Black and Indigenous people in the "political unconscious" of mainstream America.

White America hates us, then, because we are not born to white mothers. And so does apartheid Israel.

This is exactly like the difference between Donald Trump and Joe Biden, both lovers of Israel for the same reason and haters of Arab Palestinians.

Hendrik Verwoerd, Ariel Sharon, and some ideologues and politicians of World War II must be applauding with joy in their graves.

December 30, 2023

ON THE GAZA "SHOAH" AND THE "BANALITY OF EVIL"

> The reality of concentration camps resembles nothing so much as medieval pictures of Hell.
>
> —Hannah Arendt, *Eichmann in Jerusalem*

In February 2008, Matan Vilnai, then Israel's deputy defence minister, threatened the Palestinians of Gaza with a "holocaust."* "They will bring upon themselves a bigger shoah because we will use all our might to defend ourselves," he said in an interview for the Israeli army radio station, using the Hebrew word for holocaust.

It is important to recall this statement today as activists and analysts are being berated for comparing what is happening now to the people of Gaza to what European Jews suffered at the hands of the Nazis last century.

The word "shoah" is never used in Israel outside discussions of the Nazi extermination of Jews during World War II. Many Israelis, especially Zionists, have a serious problem with people using it to describe other genocides.

Yet, the deputy minister decided to threaten the Palestinians with a "shoah." It is clear he knew what he was referring to and he did not mince his words.

In December 2008, ten months after Vilnai's interview, the IOF launched a massive military onslaught on the Gaza Strip that lasted twenty-two days. Israel killed more than fourteen hundred people in this onslaught, the overwhelming majority of whom were children and women.

At the time, no one referred to the prohibited word. No one

* Originally published in a slightly different form in Haidar Eid, "On the Gaza 'Shoah' and the 'Banality of Evil,'" Opinion, *Electronic Intifada,* December 30, 2023, aljazeera.com. Reprinted with permission from the publisher.

dared to compare the military operation, grotesquely dubbed "Cast Lead," to the "shoah."

The so-called international community did nothing to protect Palestinian civilians. Just as it did nothing in the late 1930s, when it stood aside and watched idly, refusing to give shelter to the innocent civilians fleeing slaughter at the hands of the Nazi monster regime.

The Nazi war criminals acted with full impunity for a long period of time, relying on the support of ordinary Germans and the indifference of the "international community," who facilitated what the late philosopher Hannah Arendt called "the banality of evil."

Because of this, the Nazis felt at ease repeating the same crimes again and again. What Nazi officers did then looked "terrifyingly normal." As Arendt described the actions of one Nazi bureaucrat: he committed crimes "under circumstances that made it well-nigh impossible for him to know or to feel that he was doing wrong." The Nazis killed and afterwards felt no remorse whatsoever.

Nowadays, we would describe this as the normalization of war crimes and crimes against humanity. In Palestine, we are currently observing the normalization of genocide, ethnic cleansing, and apartheid.

Because the 2008 bloodbath committed by apartheid Israel was not taken seriously by the UN, the UN Security Council, the European Union, and the Arab and Muslim worlds, the besieging and slaughter of the Palestinians of Gaza in a concentration camp became "normal," or as Arendt would call it, "banal."

As a result, Israel found it easy to repeated the bloodbath in 2012, 2014, 2021, and today in 2023—all while maintaining the hermetic, medieval siege imposed in 2006. The mass killing of civilians as well as the cutting off of electricity, food, water, medicine, internet, communications, and other essential goods and services all became "normal." The Palestinians of Gaza are, after all, "human animals"—as the current Israeli defence minister, Yoav Gallant, put it frankly—and their deaths do not cause any remorse.

In normalizing genocidal violence, Israel has been aided and abetted by the colonial West. This is hardly surprising given Western countries' own track record of waging wars all over the world, from Asia to Africa to Latin America, destroying in the process Indigenous cultures and civilizations. These countries have committed heinous crimes as part of the white man's "civilizing mission."

In the Arab world, they have also maintained an imperialist project that has had two aims: one, protecting Western interests in guarding oil fields and crushing the rising nationalist sentiments; and two, managing the liberal guilt complex regarding the worst pogrom committed in the twentieth century, namely the "shoah."

This is why the Gaza "shoah" is being tolerated. The brown-skinned Palestinians of Gaza are not weighing on the Western liberal conscience and the "banal" deaths of 21,000 Palestinians at the hands of a genocidal army do not threaten Western interests in the Arab world. Hence, the failure of the UN Security Council to enforce a total ceasefire in Gaza.

So, are we to understand that Israel's genocide of Gaza is acceptable, even "normal," for the West? That the UN Security Council doesn't see the urgency of a total ceasefire now? That the UN Security Council is only an extension of the US Department of State?

Sadly, the answer to all these questions is yes.

That we find ourselves in this genocidal reality today does not mean that there is no possibility of another world order with a better UN, where all votes are equal. The pro-Palestinian rallies attended by millions of people who have taken to the streets in the US, the UK, France, South Africa, Spain, Morocco, Indonesia, Malaysia, Yemen, Jordan, Spain, Italy, Chile, Argentina, Colombia, and elsewhere and the conscionable decisions taken by the governments of Belize, Bolivia, Colombia, Chile, and South Africa, among others, show that the world wants and can be different.

It is not too difficult to imagine a near future where there is equality and real respect for the human rights of all human beings regardless of race, religion, sex, and ethnicity.

German poet Bertolt Brecht had this to say in one of the darkest times of human history:

In the dark times
Will there also be singing?
Yes, there will also be singing.
About the dark times.

January 12, 2024

FROM A PALESTINIAN IN GAZA, THANK YOU SOUTH AFRICA!

South Africa has had enough of the world's deafening silence on apartheid Israel's ongoing genocide of Palestinians in the Gaza Strip.*

The unprecedented number of war crimes and crimes against humanity Israel committed in the besieged coastal enclave in the past three months with complete impunity has put the credibility of international law at stake and sprung South Africa into action. Its top legal minds compiled an eighty-four-page document detailing evidence of these crimes and launched a landmark case at the International Court of Justice (ICJ) accusing Israel of committing genocide in contravention of the 1948 Genocide Convention.

This is music to Palestinian ears. No other country, Arab or Muslim, has ever dared cross this "red line" before. After all, this is Israel, the colonial West's spoiled baby—the one project it insisted on keeping alive after the end of the era of colonialism, camouflaging it with slogans of the Enlightenment and arming it with its best weapons. Every state on earth is undoubtedly aware of Israel's crimes, but none dares hold it to account in fear of what its colonial patrons may do in response.

Thankfully, post-apartheid South Africa eventually said "enough is enough" and took Israel to the top court of the United Nations. The nation that defeated a ruthless apartheid regime and built a multiracial, democratic state in its place recognized how the international community's silence is paving the way for Israel's deadly excesses, and it took an important step to put an end to it.

Indeed, charging Israel with the crime of genocide at the ICJ

* Originally published in a slightly different form in Haidar Eid, "From a Palestinian in Gaza, Thank You South Africa!" Opinion, *Al-Jazeera*, January 12, 2024, aljazeera.com. Reprinted with permission from the publisher.

could bring an end to Israel's impunity, create the conditions for a much-needed military embargo, and leave Israel isolated on the world stage. Even more importantly, South Africa's case could lead to provisional measures that include an immediate ceasefire and the entry of sufficient humanitarian aid into Gaza. These measures are urgently needed because every day people are dying in their thousands in the Strip. More than 23,000 people have already perished, and thousands more are missing under the rubble. About 70 percent of the victims of this horror have been women and children.

I happen to be both Palestinian and South African and a survivor of the Gaza genocide. I've lost many relatives, friends, colleagues, students, and neighbours to Israel's violence over the years.

In Gaza, I survived five attacks or, more accurately, massacres by apartheid Israel from 2008 to 2023. I've also experienced first-hand the consequences of the deadly siege it has imposed on the Strip since 2006. My entire neighbourhood was flattened by air strikes in the first week of the ongoing genocide. And I've been displaced four times since then.

Like every other inhabitant of this coastal enclave, I lived through the same dark scenario with every massacre: Israel decided to "mow the lawn," the so-called international community conveniently looked the other way and, for many long days and nights, we faced the world's most immoral army alone—an army that has hundreds of nuclear warheads and thousands of trigger-happy soldiers armed with Merkava tanks, F-16s, Apache helicopters, naval gunships, and phosphorous bombs. Once the massacre was over, everything returned to "normal," and Israel continued to kill us slowly with a suffocating siege that keeps our children malnourished, water contaminated, and nights dark. And in the many iterations of this deadly cycle that we lived through, at no point did we receive a single word of sympathy or support from the Bidens, Sunaks, Macrons, and von der Leyens of this world.

All these massacres committed with impunity made it glaringly obvious that apartheid Israel has the unequivocal backing of the white, "liberal" West to do as it pleases with Gaza and its people. These massacres were the dress rehearsals for the genocide that is under way today. They showed Israel that it can commit war crimes and crimes against humanity without receiving any sanction or condemnation from the international community. After all, no one said anything in 2008, 2012, 2014, and 2021, so why should it be any different now? This is the logic that has allowed Israel's leaders to be so open in the past few months about their intentions to "exterminate" Palestinians in Gaza.

Indeed, since the beginning of this latest massacre, this genocide, a wide range of Israeli officials from the president and the prime minister to prominent members of the government, media, and civil society have clearly voiced their intent for genocide. Just last week, Israeli Heritage Minister Amichai Eliyahu, who had previously said dropping a nuclear bomb on the Gaza Strip is "an option," urged Israel to find ways that are "more painful than death" to force Palestinians to leave the Strip.[33]

Israel's intent to commit genocide in Gaza may be more clear today than ever before, but it is in no way new. Back in 2004, Arnon Soffer, head of the National Defence College of the Israeli Offensive Forces and an adviser to then-prime minister Ariel Sharon, had already spelled out the desired results of Israel's unilateral disengagement from Gaza in an interview with the Israeli newspaper *Jerusalem Post*:

> When 1.5 million people live in a closed-off Gaza, it's going to be a human catastrophe. Those people will become even bigger animals than they are today . . . The pressure at the border will be awful. It's going to be a terrible war. So if we want to remain alive, we will have to kill and kill and kill. All day, every day . . . If we don't kill, we will cease to exist . . . Unilateral separation doesn't guarantee "peace." It guarantees a Zionist-Jewish state with an overwhelming majority of Jews.

Now, twenty years after Soffer revealed Israel's intention to "kill and kill and kill" in the Strip, Gaza is truly dying. People are being killed, maimed, starved, and displaced en masse before the eyes of the world's nations in what tragically has become the first globally watched genocide in history.

We, Palestinians, will not forget the sickening cowardice of the so-called international community, which has allowed and enabled this genocide. We will not forget how the nations of the world stood idly by as Israel's racist leaders openly claimed that we, the indigenous people of Palestine, are the "Amalek"—the foe that, according to the Torah, God ordered the ancient Israelites to commit genocide against—and embarked on a racist, inhuman quest to "annihilate" all of us.

But we will never forget what South Africa did for us either. We will not forget how it showed us unwavering support and bravely took a stand for us at the World Court when even our own brothers have turned their backs on us in fear. We will always remember how it linked our struggle, our most basic human rights, to global justice and reminded the international community of our humanity.

Israel's ongoing genocide in Gaza, being committed out in the open and with impunity, has ushered in the end of the Western-led, rules-based international order. By bravely standing up for what is right and taking Israel to the ICJ, however, South Africa showed us that another world is possible: a world where no state is above the law, most heinous crimes like genocide and apartheid are never accepted, and the peoples of the world stand together shoulder to shoulder against injustice.

Thank you, South Africa!

January 26, 2024

ICJ ISRAEL DECISION

A New World Order in the Making

Now that we have heard the interim judgment the ICJ delivered in South Africa's genocide case against Israel, we can confidently say a new world order is in the making.*

The World Court confirmed today that South Africa's charge under the Genocide Convention that "Israel has engaged in, is engaging in and risks further engaging in genocidal acts against the Palestinian people in Gaza" is "plausible." It has further ruled that Israel must "take all measures" to avoid acts of genocide in Gaza. The court has stopped short of calling for an immediate and permanent ceasefire, which has already been demanded by an absolute majority of world nations. Still, most of the "provisional measures" called for by the Republic of South Africa have been endorsed by the court. It is difficult to see how Israel can implement these measures and fulfill its obligations under the Genocide Convention without agreeing to a ceasefire.

There is no indication, of course, that Israel has any intention of heeding the court's provisions. In fact, since the ICJ heard South Africa's case two weeks ago, Israel has doubled down on its genocidal acts in Gaza.

In the past twenty-four hours alone, it carried out twenty-one mass killings, murdering 200 and injuring 370 civilians. So Israel's message to the court, and the world at large, is clear: It does not care for the opinion, demands, or "measures" of any international institution—legal or political. It will do as it pleases.

All in all, more than 1 percent of the population of Gaza has been killed and another 2.2 percent has been injured in the past

* Originally published in a slightly different form in Haidar Eid, "ICJ Israel Decision: A New World Order in the Making," Opinion, *Al-Jazeera,* January 26, 2024, aljazeera.com. Reprinted with permission from the publisher.

three months. Most of the enclave has been destroyed, and almost all of its more than two million residents have been displaced. The relentless siege, coupled with the deliberate targeting of hospitals, led to the collapse of the healthcare system. Medical services are all but nonexistent and people are dying of famine and disease, including hepatitis A and Leishmania. Even the smallest of injuries can prove to be a death sentence, as it is extremely difficult to maintain hygiene and prevent infections. Hundreds of women had miscarriages and many others died in childbirth due to lack of medical care.

In this context, it is no surprise that the World Court has found it "plausible" that Israel may be committing a genocide in Gaza. But, given its lack of interest in complying with international law—and the unconditional support it enjoys from the West—there is little reason to expect it to alter its conduct due to the court's damning interim ruling.

So why did South Africa take Israel to the ICJ, and why does today's ruling really matter?

As affirmed by South Africa, "Israel's genocidal acts" must be understood "within the broader context of Israel's 75-year apartheid." Israel has committed many violations of international law since 1948, including war crimes and crimes against humanity. Its apartheid regime and illegal occupation denied the most basic human rights of the Palestinians for nearly a century. It passed a racist nation-state law that makes "the right to exercise national self-determination" in Israel "unique to the Jewish people," establishes Hebrew as Israel's official language, and establishes "Jewish settlement as a national value" and mandates that the state "will labor to encourage and promote its establishment and development."

After ethnically cleansing most of historical Palestine of its indigenous population through massacres and theft in 1948, it went on to imprison the population of Gaza within the Strip, committing what brave Israeli historian Ilan Pappé defined in his latest book, *The Biggest Prison on Earth: A History of Gaza and the Occupied Territories*, as "ethnic cleansing by other means." "[Palestinians in Gaza] are contained inside their own areas, but do not have to be counted in the overall national demographics since they cannot freely move, develop or expand, nor do they have any basic civil and human rights," explained Pappé.

Since the moment of its very inception, Israel worked to eliminate the indigenous population of Palestine through ethnic cleansing, apartheid, ghettoization, and segregation. And now, it is committing the very first livestreamed and globally watched genocide in human history.

How could South Africa, a nation that itself experienced the worst of settler colonialism, ethnic cleansing, and racial segregation, a nation that has successfully destroyed a vicious apartheid regime and replaced it with a multiracial, multicultural, progressive democracy, remain silent in the face of Israel's crimes?

It could not.

South Africans recognized that taking no action on Israel's continuing genocide in Gaza would have meant no lesson had been learned from the Sharpeville and Soweto massacres, from everything they endured under settler-colonial rule, from years of apartheid.

They realized that now that Israel's occupation and oppression reached their genocidal climax, the international community no longer has the luxury of waiting, issuing statements, and hoping for the best. Every single minute of inaction brings more loss, more death, and more despair to Palestinians.

So they took action—they took Israel to the highest court of the world and accused it of committing the world's most heinous crime: genocide.

Israel may not heed the court's rulings and provisions, but South Africa's historic stance will still have consequences. As stated by the Department of International Relations and Cooperation of South Africa after the ICJ's interim decision:

> Third States are now on notice of the existence of a serious risk of genocide against the Palestinian people in Gaza. They must, therefore, also act independently and immediately to prevent genocide by Israel and to ensure that they are not themselves in violation of the Genocide Convention, including by aiding or assisting in the commission of genocide. This necessarily

imposes an obligation on all States to cease funding and facilitating Israel's military actions, which are plausibly genocidal.

With this case, South Africa has put not only Israel but the entirety of the global justice system on trial. This case is a major turning point for humanity because it marks the first time in history when a Global South country bravely crossed a red line drawn by the colonial West and demanded its favourite settler colony, Israel, be held to account for the crimes it has long been committing against an indigenous people. Today, thanks to South Africa, the entire colonial West and its centuries-long history of theft, dispossession, and injustice is on trial at the World Court.

Future generations will remember January 26, 2024, as the day on which the world has finally decided to hold a genocide state, and its powerful backers, accountable for repeated, long-standing violations of international law. Yes, a new world order is in the making.

May 1, 2024

THE GENOCIDE IN GAZA WILL ALSO BE THE END OF ISRAEL

It has been 207 days since the beginning of the Gaza genocide.* Over 34,200 civilians have been killed, including 14,500 children, and 10,000 women. Over 10,000 people are still buried under the rubble. Mass graves have been uncovered at hospitals in the north and the south of Gaza. At the time of writing, hundreds of dead bodies have just been discovered in a huge mass grave at Nasser Hospital in Khan Younis. Mothers are still trying to identify the bodies of their sons and daughters. Two thousand people are still missing.

Euro-Med Human Rights Monitor has documented 140 mass and unmarked graves so far in Gaza. The barbarity by Israel is unprecedented. Among the deceased in the mass graves at al-Shifa and Nasser hospitals, some people had been stripped of their clothes and buried with their hands tied. According to World Health Organization Director-General Tedros Adhanom Ghebreyesus, a child is killed every ten minutes in Gaza on average. Ghebreyesus paints a gloomy picture: "Nowhere and no one is safe."

Almost all Gazans have been displaced, waiting for the day when they will return home as a first step towards their return to the towns and villages from which they and their parents were ethnically cleansed in 1948. Now, nothing is left. The beautiful coastal Strip is no longer recognizable. Two-thirds of its houses have been destroyed; roads, hospitals, schools, universities, factories, shops, cemeteries, libraries, mosques, churches, restaurants, stadiums, farms, water wells, electricity generators . . . all have been erased.

Yet that does not seem to be enough for genocidal Israel,

* Originally published in a slightly different form in Haidar Eid, "The Genocide in Gaza Will Also Be the End of Israel," Opinion, *Mondoweiss*, May 1, 2024, mondoweiss.net. Reprinted with permission from the publisher.

the United States of America, and the colonial West! They have decided to starve the people of Gaza by closing all the crossings and banning all kinds of food, clean water, and medicines. Even the UNRWA has been defunded—despite an independent UN commission saying that Israel had failed to offer evidence for its smears against the aid agency—and for one reason only: to kill more Gazans.

The decision taken by major colonial powers to defund UNRWA has led the Lemkin Institute for Genocide Prevention to sound the alarm and state: "[This] represents a shift by several countries from potential complicity in genocide to direct involvement in engineered famine."

It is then a clear intent to get rid of the indigenous population of Palestine. In 1948, heads of the Zionist gangs made the mistake of "not finishing the job," according to Israel's leading right-wing historian Benny Morris, who has recently written an op-ed for the *New York Times* calling for the slaughter (genocide) of the Palestinians of Rafah: "It's crucial for Israel to conquer Rafah."[34] Just like that!

In her report for the UN Human Rights Council, UN Special Rapporteur on the occupied Palestinian territories Francesca Albanese wrote:

> [There are] reasonable grounds to believe that the threshold indicating the commission of the following acts of genocide against Palestinians in Gaza has been met: killing members of the group; causing serious bodily or mental harm to groups' members; and deliberately inflicting on the group conditions of life calculated to bring about its physical destruction in whole or in part.

In fact, the threshold for genocide by Israel against the Palestinians was met years ago. Although the recent campaign in Gaza leaves little doubt, Zionism has always been a genocidal campaign against the Palestinian people. The Palestinian has become the Other of the flourishing white Ashkenazi "self," whose very existence necessitates the annihilation of the "nonexistent" natives.[35]

And why has the colonial West decided, through Israel, to carry out these horrific crimes? Perhaps a hint can be found in Edward Said's *Orientalism*, where he argues that "the major component in European culture is precisely what made [Western civilization] hegemonic both in and outside Europe: the idea of European identity as a superior one in comparison with all the non-European peoples and cultures."[36] Compare the colonial West's reaction to the Ukrainian crisis to what is happening in Gaza. Palestinians at the end of the day are not part of "us," whereas Ukrainians are white Europeans.

Apartheid Israel, then, is committing genocide because it is a settler colony. But, as argued by some critical historians (Ilan Pappé and Joseph Massad among them), the final years of all settler colonies are marked by more protracted savagery by the colonizers, including genocide. The realization that the loss of settler-colonial privilege is close at hand drives colonial forces to use the most savage methods to defeat the revolt of the indigenous people. It happened in Algeria, South Africa, Zimbabwe, Namibia, and other formerly colonized countries where the colonizing powers carried out massacres even as colonialism was in its death throes.

The more resistance the colonized indigenous population shows, the more brutal the colonizer becomes. Genocidal Israel's fascist political elite cannot tolerate any form of resistance on the part of native Palestinians. So far, at least 608 Israeli soldiers have been killed by Palestinian fighters—this is unprecedented in the history of the "conflict." And there are consequences that Palestinian civilians are being forced to pay. This was the same logic in all settler colonies on their deathbed. But the horrific question remains: How long will the genocide continue? And how many more dead bodies of innocent Palestinian children, men, and women does the international community want to see in order to act?

June 9, 2024

MY NUSEIRAT

> In the next war, we will alert populations in Lebanon and in Gaza the moment tensions begin that they must leave . . . In the face of these threats, we will respond with an extremely significant counterattack that will include targeting rockets, missiles and weapons, whether in open areas, or adjacent to and inside buildings.
>
> —IOF Chief of Staff Avi Kochavi

I was born in the Nuseirat refugee camp; all my siblings were born there too.* My father, together with my sister and brother, are buried in two of its cemeteries. Almost the entire Eid clan still lives there, and those butchered by genocidal Israel's killing machine are buried there. Hundreds of my students are from there. I know almost every single street of the camp; I am familiar with the faces of its residents, all of whom are refugees from towns and villages erased by apartheid Israel in 1948.

Nuseirat, one of Gaza's eight refugee camps, has become a major component of my national and class consciousness, a place of both destitution and revolution. In the early 1970s, I was a small child when I heard of the clashes between the fida'iyyin, our supermen, and the Zionist "villains." Stories of heroism and martyrdom in defence of the camp and a lost country called Falasteen were discussed by family, relatives, neighbours, and friends—all refugees from the south of the "Land of Sad Oranges," as referred to by our intellectual giant, Ghassan Kanafani. A connection was created by the village of Zarnouqa, from which my parents were expelled by Zionist thugs together with thousands of other villagers in 1948, and Nuseirat. The Zarnouqa/Nuseirat dialect became the correct

* Originally published in a slightly different form in Haidar Eid, "My Nuseirat," Opinion, *Mondoweiss,* June 9, 2024, mondoweiss.net. Reprinted with permission from the publisher.

form of spoken Arabic for me; its *bortoqal*,* I was told, were the best in the whole wide world (sometimes the speaker would acknowledge "second to Jaffa's"!) Those orange orchards were replanted around Nuseirat until apartheid Israel decided to uproot them all during the First Intifada of the late 1980s and early 90s.

I am writing this piece hours after genocidal Israel killed 274 and injured more than 400 beautiful Nuseiraties, many of whom are my relatives, friends, and students—only to rescue four of its captives. Sixty-four of the victims were children, and fifty-seven were women. Those who were brutally murdered were either going to or coming back from Camp Souk, having their breakfast, playing in the street, going to the Al-Awda hospital, cooking food, and visiting relatives and friends; that is, the timing was chosen carefully in order to kill as many people as possible.

When will genocidal Biden be satisfied? How many more children have to lose limbs or be killed? How many mothers have to be murdered or lose their little ones to convince the colonial West, led by the United States, that it is time to have a ceasefire? Obviously, the 36,800 killed, including 15,000 children and 11,000 women, with more than 11,000 under the rubble, are not enough. How about the destruction of 70 percent of the entire Gaza Strip? The killing of hundreds of its academics, doctors, and journalists? The erasure of whole families from the civil registry? The closure of its seven gates? The starving to death of those who refuse to leave?

No, not enough.

Gaza is being annihilated in real-time in front of the eyes of the world. In fact, Gaza has ushered in the beginning of the end of "human rights" as defined and monopolized by the colonial West. Neither the ICJ nor the ICC or the UNGA and its Security Council have been able to stop the genocide and protect my Nuseirat. And why? Only because some brown native Palestinians managed to break out of Gaza after over a decade and a half of living under a total land, air, and sea blockade in the largest open-air prison on earth! How dare they shatter Israel and the colonial West's image of military invincibility.

* oranges

Nuseirat is a microcosm of the genocide. The lives of 4 white Ashkenazi Israelis are equivalent to the lives of 274 native mothers, doctors, and children. The white world is celebrating this "victory" regardless of the "collateral damage," as long as the victims are not like "us," the white gods of this unjust world.

The Nuseirat massacre is not a moment of victory after which Benjamin Netanyahu and his gang of fascist thugs can call it a day. There will be more massacres committed by the same bloodthirsty colonizers. But Nuseirat, like all massacres committed by colonialists, whether in Algeria, South Africa, Ireland, or other settler colonies, will be a signpost in our long walk to freedom. And only those who stand on the right side of history can read the signs.

June 28, 2024

WAR ON GAZA

The World Has Abandoned Us. What Can We Do?

The bitter reality for Palestinians in Gaza is that we are alone, beleaguered, under siege, and abandoned even by those who are supposed to be our brethren.*

Nearly nine months of barbaric massacres have claimed the lives of more than 37,000 Palestinians, many of whom are women and children. The victims have included doctors and nurses on duty in hospitals, university students, and people doing household chores.

Entire families have been slaughtered in broad daylight, amid Israel's systematic destruction of thousands of homes in Gaza. Another 10,000 people are missing, believed to be dead and buried under the rubble.

And yet, the US still blames Palestinians while criticizing international courts for trying to hold Israel to account for its ongoing genocide.

Palestinians have been left alone to defend themselves against the onslaught of a state backed by the world's biggest army. The US has supplied Israel with billions of dollars in weaponry, including bombs and fighter jets, to prolong its war.

Meanwhile, the humanitarian tragedy in Gaza has reached unimaginable levels. The few remaining hospitals are struggling to cope with the influx of injured civilians. Neighbouring Arab regimes have done nothing more than issue timid statements of condemnation while mediating between oppressor and oppressed.

Indeed, Arab regimes have let Palestinians down since 1948, through a combination of cowardice and hypocrisy. They have

* Originally published in a slightly different form in Haidar Eid, "War on Gaza: The World Has Abandoned Us. What Can We Do?" Opinion, *Middle East Eye*, June 28, 2024, middleeasteye.net. Reprinted with permission from the publisher.

failed to bring an end to Israel's seventeen-year siege on Gaza, or even to offer meaningful solidarity with the Palestinian people, who are at the receiving end of Israel's brutal military offensive.

Aiding the Oppressor

We have exhausted ourselves trying to figure out the possible ways of achieving democratic political change. As the Gaza genocide drags on, we have not seen any practical translation by Arab states of the solidarity shown by some of their peoples with Palestine.

Once again, the international community, United Nations, European Union, and Arab leaders have remained largely silent about Israel's ongoing atrocities. This puts them on Israel's side.

Thousands of corpses of women and children have failed to convince them of the need to act. Palestinians have realized that they have only one tenable option: popular power, which is the only force capable of tackling the huge asymmetry of power in the Palestinian-Israeli conflict.

For the past seventeen years, the two choices for Palestinians in Gaza have been to die slowly amid Israel's suffocating blockade or to fight for dignity—their own and that of future generations. Many have chosen to fight, departing from years of self-deception that portrayed subjugation to the occupier as a fait accompli.

In this context, proposed ceasefire initiatives do not take into account Israel's objectives in the Gaza war: to eliminate the largest number of Palestinians possible by targeting civilian homes and infrastructure and to remove any potential source of resistance to Israeli occupation in the open-air extermination camp we know as Gaza.

Root Causes

Instead, the initiatives that have been put forward equate Palestinian resistance with the Israeli regime of systematic oppression, apartheid, and settler colonialism. It seems as though the world expects Palestinians to simply accept their slow death without any form of rebellion.

But Palestinians, in Gaza and elsewhere, will not oblige.

Any agreement that does not lead to an immediate ceasefire, the lifting of Israel's devastating blockade, and the permanent reopening of all border crossings in a manner that allows the entry of fuel, medicine, and other basic goods will not be acceptable to the people of Gaza. The deal must also provide for the withdrawal of Israeli forces without delay.

The current war cannot be seen in isolation from the root causes of the situation in Gaza: Israel's settler-colonial enterprise, occupation, apartheid, and ethnic cleansing. This conflict must be situated within our demand for the Palestinian right of return to the lands from which hundreds of thousands were driven out in 1948. Two-thirds of the people of Gaza are refugees who have this right under international law.

From Rafah, to Nuseirat, to Jabalia and the rest of Gaza, we have reached a pivotal moment in Palestinian history. Gaza yearns for a leadership that rises to the occasion, recognizing the idea of Palestine from the river to the sea.

Any talk of improving our conditions of oppression—and even this is seen as too much for us—in light of the great sacrifices that have been made, is a betrayal of Gaza's martyrs. We need to start discussing radical solutions to move beyond the status quo, and we need to adopt a clear slogan: end the occupation, end apartheid, and end settler colonialism. If this happens, all the lives lost in Gaza would not have been lost in vain.

July 13, 2024

NOW THE ANEMONE FLOWERS WILL DECORATE HIS GRAVE

I am writing this while the terrorist IOF are attacking the Tuffah, Daraj, and Shuja'iyya neighbourhoods in Gaza.* They are forcing hundreds of thousands of people out of their homes towards Remal in the west of Gaza City, which itself is under heavy bombardment. Hundreds of bodies are scattered in the streets. No Red Cross or Red Crescent relief or medical workers are allowed into the areas to provide medical attention or essential supplies.

A few days ago, I received the news of the martyrdom of Saadi Mdoukh, our friend, music producer, and the videographer who produced our best video clips (Mariyamiya and Mweil El Hawa). He was in his late 20s–early 30s, full of ambitions, dreams, and hopes. He was killed together with members of his family in the very locations where we shot the second video. He said when we filmed the video that he chose this location because it was "full of the anemone flowers which grow on martyrs' graves." Now the anemone flowers will decorate his own.

What did we—Saadi, Reziq (the composer of the song), and I—talk about that day? What was Saadi's reaction when the word "martyr" was uttered? There is a strong belief among Palestinians that martyrs experience a strange feeling before they are killed. They feel something is going to happen to them, but they don't know what it is. Is this why Saadi suggested that we shoot the video clip in that place, among the anemone flowers? Did he want to get more intimate with them, the anemones?

His martyrdom coincided with the fifty-second anniversary of the assassination of one of the most revolutionary, talented writers

* Originally published in a slightly different form in Haidar Eid, "Now the Anemone Flowers Will Decorate His Grave," Opinion, *Mondoweiss*, July 13, 2024, mondoweiss.net. Reprinted with permission from the publisher.

in Palestine, Ghassan Kanafani. Kanafani wrote about ordinary Palestinians living their abnormal, miserable lives in the Diaspora after the 1948 Nakba. He wrote about the Palestinians' heroic resistance to genocidal Israel's multitiered system of oppression. Towards the end of *All That Is Left to You* and *Returning to Haifa* (both of which I taught at what used to be Al-Aqsa University before Israel bombed it) the choice is clear: resistance is existence. If you refrain from resisting your occupier, you die a meaningless, miserable death, a fate the heroes of *Men in the Sun* could not avoid.

But the people of Gaza, two-thirds of whom are refugees from Israel's 1948 genocide of the Palestinians, and entitled to their right of return to their towns and villages, have made up their minds. In the face of one of the worst genocides ever committed in real-time in front of the eyes of a deaf world, the people of Gaza have decided to challenge Israel's myth of invincibility. Ironically, just as the colonial West, namely Europe and North America, looked the other way when the Nazis were perpetrating the Holocaust, the so-called international community is finding a way to do nothing as apartheid Israel continues to slaughter Palestinian children and women in Gaza.

Palestinian lives do not matter at all. If they did then why has this unprecedented genocide, following seventeen years of an incremental genocide while Gaza was placed under siege, been allowed to last for ten months? Why have over 38,200 Palestinians, 70 percent of whom are women and children, 95 percent of whom are civilians, lost their precious lives?

The fascist minister of national security of apartheid Israel, Itamar Ben-Gvir, summed it up when he recently tried to have a new law passed that would allow Israeli prisons to summarily execute all Palestinian prisoners without trial: "All Palestinian prisoners are to be executed and shot in the head"![37] Indoctrinated Israelis, supported by Western leaders, do not accept Palestinians as equal citizens because they are accustomed to believing in their own superiority as a white colonial society.

The dilemma revolves around maintaining Israel as a state for Jews only while another people lives in the land. Gentile Palestinians, especially the dark-skinned refugees of Gaza, are expected to ignore the past and their own suffering, to be content with the crumbs of bread offered to them while being kept inside the walls of the Gaza zoo, which has now been turned by Israel into an extermination camp.

I am thinking of Saadi and the thousands of young men whose lives have been cut short; what did they want? The great revolutionary intellectual and freedom fighter Amilcar Cabral might answer me: "Always bear in mind that the people are not fighting for ideas, for the things in anyone's head. They are fighting to win material benefits, to live better and in peace, to see their lives go forward, to guarantee the future of their children."[38]

Saadi, like Khalil Abu Yahya and Tasnim Thabet (my former students who were killed together with their families), wanted to live a better life; they wanted to send their kids to school, get a higher education, find better jobs, become teachers, directors, movie makers, and live in peace.

Woe unto us, *ya weili*, because they were not allowed to live.

THE ONE YEAR ANNIVERSARY OF OCTOBER 7

Personal Reflections

When I was asked by the editors of *Mondoweiss* to write my reflections on the one year anniversary of the October 7 invasion of Gaza by Israel, while the genocide continues with no end in sight, I thought of all the hundreds of relatives, comrades, friends, colleagues, and students who have been killed by Israel over the last year—each and every one of them!* From five-month-old Ellen Eid to my former students Khail Abu Yahya, Tasneem Thabet, and Reem El Farra to my friend and orthopaedic surgeon Dr. Adnan El Bursh, my colleague Refaat El Areer, my two cousins Takween and Haifaa and their families, my nephews Fouad and Mustapha and their whole families.

I thought of writing all the names, but that will not be enough to do them justice. I have tried to count how many people I personally have lost, a task I do not wish on my worst enemy. I even wrote a while ago that "I've lost count of the number of the people I have lost!" They have become torches on our long walk to freedom from occupation, colonialism, and apartheid.

But the comrades in *Mondoweiss* want also an analysis of the current situation; they want to know whether I am hopeful or not, they want to know about the way forward from here. And I am not sure whether I am able to respond to these almost impossible questions! Writing a PhD thesis was like a picnic compared to answering these questions. Whatever I write will not satisfy me, but despair is a luxury we Palestinians cannot afford! Last century, our late novelist Emile Habibi coined the term "Pessoptomism" to express the status quo of the Palestinian people, a term that

* Originally published in a slightly different form in Haidar Eid, "A Vision for Freedom Is More Important Than Ever," Opinion, *Mondoweiss*, October 13, 2024, mondoweiss.net. Reprinted with permission from the publisher.

embodies the Gramscian notion of "the pessimism of the intellect and the optimism of the will."

I, together with my family, have been displaced four times, three of them in Gaza itself, until I was evacuated by the South African government from Rafah in the second month of the genocide, December 2023. I have been living with a survivor's guilt complex since then.

So much has been written on the events of October 7, and more will be added. I have my own take too, a position that goes against the decontextualized analysis of the mainstream media, which happens to be white and colonial and which tends to fully endorse the Israeli narrative. I fully agree with the remarks made by the UN Secretary-General Antonio Guterres when he addressed the Security Council on the October 24, 2023: "It is important to also recognize the attacks by Hamas did not happen in a vacuum." He went on to elaborate, "The Palestinian people have been subjected to 56 years of suffocating occupation. They have seen their land steadily devoured by settlements and plagued by violence; their economy stifled; their people displaced and their homes demolished. Their hopes for a political solution to their plight have been vanishing." The difference between my position and this one is the number of years of oppression; the secretary-general is surely aware of the Nakba that took place in 1948. It is not fifty-six years of oppression but rather seventy-six years of ethnic cleansing and settler colonialism culminating in the ongoing genocide livestreamed in front of the eyes of an indifferent world. Antonio Guterres knows very well that two-thirds of the Palestinians of Gaza are refugees entitled to the UNGA Resolution 194, which calls for their return to the towns and villages from which they were ethnically cleansed in 1948.

This is precisely why genocidal Israel has decided to "finish the job," to use the words of Israel's most celebrated fascist historian and genocidaire Benny Morris. Gaza is a constant reminder of the existence of native Palestinians on the land as refugees waiting to return. This, however, is happening within a classical settler-colonial world of Manichean binary of violence premised on false categories of good and evil, light and dark, and so on.

But we ought to ask where this tit for tat situation is heading. How will Israel's denial of Palestinian rights, and Palestinian resistance to it, end?

After seventy-six years of Israel's existence, we have arrived at the point of no return for all living in historic Palestine. It has become very obvious now that no solution to the so-called Israeli-Palestinian conflict—to use mainstream media's favourite term—can be envisaged under these terrible circumstances created by genocidal Israel in historic Palestine. Surely you cannot expect colonized Palestinians to compromise on their basic human rights.

There are two opinions, one that argues for statehood on a portion of the land of historic Palestine and does not guarantee Palestinian basic rights—and ultimately prolongs the oppression of the Palestinian people. But why are we Palestinians expected to accept solutions that take no account of the reality of our situation? This is the position adopted by mainstream political organizations in Palestine, Western countries, and a tiny section of liberal Zionism.

The second perspective argues for the implementation of international law giving Palestinians their right of return, right to equality, and ultimately their right to self-determination like any other people on the face of earth.

And, one might add, a third genocidal position is being implemented right now by apartheid Israel and expressed openly by its fascist prime minister and ministers. For them, the objectives of the ongoing genocide are:

- Reoccupying the Gaza Strip.
- Forced removal of a large portion of the population by preventing any food from entering Gaza, by bombing institutions of education and health care, and by obliterating the right to security and work.
- Slicing the Strip onto cantons like in the West Bank and invading and carrying out regular massacres inside these cantons.
- Creating a loyal, local government.

But the colonial West refuses to see the objective conditions of being subjugated to occupation, settler colonialism, and apartheid. It refuses to see Gazans as human beings entitled to their basic rights like all other human beings only because they are not born to Jewish mothers. As Salman Abu Sitta reminds us on his Facebook page: There are two million Palestinian refugees in the Gaza Strip who came from 247 towns and villages in southern Palestine, expelled by Israel in 1948 through dozens of massacres. They are crammed in a concentration camp called the Gaza Strip at a density of 8000 persons/km². Its area is 1.3 percent of Palestine, or 365 km². They are now forced by Israel to move down south, then up north in the tiny Strip at a density exceeding 20,000 p/km². He goes on to ask: "Who occupies their home?" The answer? Eastern European settlers from Romania, Poland, Ukraine, and Russia. Their number is only 150,000, at a density of only 7 persons/km², one thousand times less than the owners of the land, who are the refugees in Gaza.

One also ought to ask tough questions within the historical context of the unfolding events. Would the genocide have taken place had the Oslo Accords not been signed in 1993? My position is that post-Oslo, Palestine is struggling to overcome the past because the material conditions of occupation, apartheid, and settler colonialism at present are hegemonic, but also because the intellectual conditions created by Oslo have legitimized those conditions. The accords themselves are a trojan horse that have turned out to be little more than a war machine with which we have come to make a premature "peace."

Since then, we have been searching for a form of freedom that points towards an exit from the constraints of apartheid, occupation, and settler colonialism. We stumbled upon this in the course of our struggles—a form of liberation that expresses resolute confidence in our ability to ensure a redemptive end to settler-colonial oppression, as expressed in the ideas of our critical thinkers and writers, the likes of Ghassan Kanafani and Edward Said. Unfortunately, the founders of contemporary Palestinian nationalism never grasped the form of Zionism they were dealing with when they signed the accords. That led to the spread of a form of false consciousness among a large portion of the population that Oslo would lead to "independence" for Palestinians by 1999. Yasser Arafat's arrival in Gaza in 1994 was met with the thunderous euphoria and welcome of the post-occupation (postcolonial!) world that so eagerly awaited a new promise of the future. Since then, what we have been dealing with is the sophistry of a mastery political narrative that claimed to have established peace through partition, the two-state solution!

While it is important to focus on the present, as things on the ground are getting worse every day, having a clear strategy and political vision is crucial if we want people around the globe to see what is possible. People keep asking the same question again and again: What is the future of Gaza? Can that be discussed without relating it to the future of Palestine in general? What kind of Palestine do we want to see in the future (the day after)? Is the (racist) two-state solution still possible? Can Palestinians and white Ashkenazi settlers coming from Europe share the same land, like what happened in South Africa, without dismantling apartheid and settler colonialism?

Working on this piece while Israel is indiscriminately carpet bombing my people in Gaza is extremely difficult. One source of inspiration, or rather motivation, behind these dispatches, is Edward Said's "Permission to Narrate" in which he called upon us Palestinians to take our struggle to the world of representation and historical narratives. As he argued very eloquently, the existing imbalance of political and military powers does not mean that the subaltern, the marginalized, do not possess the ability to struggle over the production of knowledge.

Sometimes I seriously wonder: Am I the only one who has been unable to read a book, watch a movie, enjoy a meal, play with my kids, since October 7?

Let me close with a quote from the late martyr Shireen Abu Akleh:

"We're in it for the long haul, keep your spirits up!"

EPILOGUE

Ethnic cleansing of Palestinians will not solve Israel's existential dilemma or even Israeli Prime Minister Benjamin Netanyahu's problems. It seems he is desperately using the genocide to remain in power and distract Israeli voters from the three cases of fraud, breach of trust, and bribery that he was indicted for after accepting hundreds of thousands of dollars' worth of bribes from Israeli companies to promote legislation that would have enriched those companies.

On the contrary, Israel's continuation of the genocide against Palestinians will only create more troubles for the surrounding Arab allies of the US in the region. These include the first two Arab states to have normalized diplomatic ties with the Jewish state—Egypt and Jordan.

Israel is now on the verge of collapse, its future as the state of Jews all over the world, a state that guarantees security and prosperity for all Jews, having been thrown into doubt not only in the West but also in Israel itself. And yet, as the Arabs watch, the Europeans look away, and the Americans nod, Israel slaughters countless more Palestinians in the hope of getting rid of all of them. Gaza is just the beginning!

The Palestinian culture of resistance has gained a tremendous momentum in the Occupied Territories; not only in Gaza, but also in Jenin, Tul Karm, Nur Shams, Balata, and Nablus in the West Bank. Where, previously, resistance operations were an exception, in the West Bank they have now become the rule. Moreover, this culture is expected to spread to the neighbouring countries. It has the potential to spread to other parts of the world, as witnessed in the protests in the US, UK, France, Italy, Morocco, Jordan, Spain, South Africa, and other parts of the globe.

As the symbol of the Intifada—the stone—made its way into global resistance literature as a form of protest against tanks, M16 bombers, and other lethal weapons used by Israel, so too has *sumud** become the response to weapons of mass destruction owned by superpowers (including Israel). In other words, resilience has become the ideal tool in the confrontation against American political and security globalization, a globalization that is biased towards genocide, oppression, dictatorship, and corruption.

There are not two sides involved in the "violence" in the Middle East. As Edward Said wrote a very long time ago, "there is a colonial state turning all its great power against a stateless people, repeatedly refugees, and dispossessed people, bereft of arms with the aim of destroying this people."

What is left for the Palestinian people after the allegedly fourth, some say third, strongest army in the world, with its navy and air force, has been bombarding all of the tiny Gaza Strip? Years of "negotiations" have created only Bantustans and extermination camps. At Camp David in 2000 when the Palestinians asked for the implementation of international law, they were accused of blowing off the then Israeli prime minister Ehud Barak's "generous" offer of continued colonization and Bantustanisation of Palestine.

Today, Palestinians have been at the receiving end of merciless assaults by Israeli troops, and reservists, hidden in their helicopters, gunships, F-16's, and tanks. What are the Palestinians to do now?

The current US government considers the killing of Palestinians by tank and plane missiles "legitimate," whereas resistance operations—conducted by youngsters living in despair as a result of the unbalanced powers—are considered to be "terrorist attacks." Netanyahu, therefore, is given the green light by the US to conduct his genocidal attacks against Palestinians whose deaths in the hundreds of thousands becomes mere "collateral damage."

The Biden-Harris administration did not have a balanced plan to resolve the crisis in the Middle East. The most spineless US secretary of state, Anthony Blinken, was trying to convince the Palestinians to accept a ceasefire based solely on Israeli conditions and without any international legitimacy. A ceasefire that would be delinked from any clear political program based on Security Council resolutions and international legitimacy that

* steadfastness, or the enduring will to resist

guarantee our right to self-determination. We will see what the Trump administration brings.

Of course, the logical outcome of this biased, even antagonistic, American position, and the lack of will to find a just solution and peace, is catastrophic. But it also means the failure of the American "anti-terror" campaign and even the dismantling of the alliance it is trying to form in the region against Russia, China, and the Islamic Republic of Iran.

Further, the American, and international, conspiracy of silence will necessitate the growth of radicalism in the region and the silencing of genuinely moderate voices. The oppressed Arabian and Islamic peoples can no longer accept the American double standards. This can be seen by the fact that the Israeli reoccupation of the already occupied West Bank and Gaza Strip has not stopped Palestinian resistance operations—on the contrary, it has intensified them. When Ariel Sharon, then Israeli minister of defence, decided to invade Lebanon in 1982, the Lebanese National and Islamic resistance emerged as a such a huge challenge that the IOF was forced to withdraw, humiliated, from South Lebanon.

Israel has won all of its previous wars against the official Arab regimes but has lost all of its onslaughts against Arab resistance and liberation movements. It will surely lose the current genocidal war against the Palestinians of Gaza and will be forced to withdraw its forces unconditionally. Arab presidents and kings are enjoying the comfort of their palaces among their wives, concubines, and slaves. The most they have come up with in defence of Palestine are tons of meaningless verbal condemnations of Israel. The generals and marshals of the Arab states have been busy condemning Israeli attacks and begging Genocide Joe to intervene and to soften his brutality while the children of Gaza sacrifice their lives for the dignity and honour of not only Palestinians but for the entire Arab nation and even humanity.

This book was not meant to only be a testimony of a Palestinian living in Gaza, a genocide survivor, but also a call for resistance inspired by those who have died fighting for their human dignity, freedom, and justice, including the late Ghassan Kanafani, whose literary and political work has inspired me since I was a child. The question Kanafani's *Men in the Sun* ends with—"Why didn't they bang on the walls of the tank?!"—essentially indicates the longing for the kind of justice and dignity all Palestinians are fighting for, since one's original land is a precondition for a decent life, free from alienation and exploitation.

The question of resistance is the real focus of Kanafani's text: resistance as a precondition for the existence of the human being who is worthy of his/her humanity and the homeland that grants him/her dignity and stability. However, by repeating the question "Why? Why? Why?," one is compelled to offer an answer. In other words, the question invites a provocative answer: banging on the sides of the tank/grave; it is death; do not accept it; move and shout. And Gazans have been banging on the walls of the Gaza concentration camp since 1948.

ACKNOWLEDGEMENTS

Here, at the mercy of time,
on these foothills at sunset
near ripped-up orchards stripped of their shadows,
we do what prisoners do,
we do what the unemployed do:
we cultivate hope.

—Mahmoud Darwish, "A State of Siege"

Pain can surprisingly bring out the best in people!

The horrific days and nights through which Israel committed the mother of all crimes in my Gaza has made me a *different* Haidar. Helplessness, horror, pain, loneliness, alienation, melancholy—but also resilience! That cocktail of mixed feelings is indescribable. Being an activist does not help me stop an American-made F-16 from targeting my birthplace, Nuseirat, or another American-made canon from shelling the houses of Jabaliya. The long, dark nights were in cahoots with apartheid Israel, both against me. Radio stations and satellite channels have been reporting constant breaking news live from the scene of different massacres. My heart and mind have been struggling really hard to take in all the news in one go. But this news has been mixed with flesh and blood; my friends' flesh and blood, my nieces', my nephews', my students', my colleagues' . . . tens of thousands of Gazans. I would like to acknowledge their inspiration; without them, it would have been impossible to compile this book.

I must also acknowledge the editors of *Mondoweiss*, *The Electronic Intifada*, *Al Jazeera*, *Middle East Eye*, One Democratic State Campaign, *Al-Shabaka*, OpenDemocracy, StopTheWall.org, SocialistWorker.org, and *The Palestine Chronicle* for their generosity and support.

Amanda Crocker, and the rest of the team at Between the Lines, and my copy editor, Candida Hadley, my comrades, have offered a tremendous amount of support.

Last but not least, and despite the little ones' constant interruption, I acknowledge my little family's presence in my life. My partner, Rifka, and my two little angels, Haifa and Salma, who have witnessed three horrific genocidal wars. To them I am eternally indebted.

NOTES

1 Ilan Pappé, *The Biggest Prison on Earth* (Oneworld Publications, 2019).

2 W. H. Auden, "September 1, 1939," in *Poetry of the Thirties*, ed. Robin Skelton (Penguin, 1964).

3 Rashid Khalidi, *Brokers of Deceit: How the U.S. Has Undermined Peace in the Middle East* (Beacon Press, 2013).

4 Edward Said, "Permission to Narrate," *Journal of Palestine Studies* 13, no. 3 (Spring 1984).

5 Ghassan Kanafani, *Men In The Sun*, trans. Hilary Kilpatrick (Three Continents Press, 1978).

6 Michel Foucault, *The History of Sexuality, Volume 1: An Introduction*, trans. Robert Hurley (Pantheon Books, 1978).

7 Frantz Fanon, *The Wretched of the Earth* (Penguin Books, 1990), 197.

8 Fanon, *Wretched of the Earth*, 178–79.

9 Edward Said, *Representations of the Intellectual* (Vintage, 1994), 9.

10 International Convention on the Suppression and Punishment of Apartheid, UNGA Resolution 3068, un.org.

11 Saree Makdisi, "A Racism Outside of Language: Israel's Apartheid," *Pambazuka News*, March 11, 2010, pambazuka.org.

12 "Hamas Military Chief Killed in Israeli Attack," *Al-Jazeera*, November 14, 2012, aljazeera.com.

13 Edward Said, *After the Last Sky* (Columbia University Press, 1998).

14 Ghassan Kanafani, *All That is Left to You* (Interlink, 2004).

15 Walter Benjamin, "The Work of Art in the Age of Mechanical Reproduction," in *Illuminations: Essays and Reflections*, ed. Hannah Arendt, trans. Harry Zohn (Schocken Books, 1968).

16 Kurtz is a character in Joseph Conrad's *Heart of Darkness* (Dover Publications, 1990).

17 "Ronnie Kasrils Speech at Israeli Apartheid Week," BDS Movement, March 20, 2009, bdsmovement.net.

18 Moshe Dayan was an Israeli war criminal who once said, "Israel must be like a mad dog, too dangerous to bother."

19 Steve Biko, *I Write What I Like,* ed. Aelred Stubs C.R. (University of Chicago Press, 2002).

20 Ilan Pappé, *The Biggest Prison on Earth: A History of the Occupied Territories* (Oneworld Publications, 2019).

21 Conal Urquhart, "Gaza on Brink of Implosion As Aid Cut-Off Starts to Bite," *The Guardian*, April 16, 2016.

22 Tovah Lazaroff, "'There Are No Innocents in Gaza,' Says Israeli Defense Minister," *Haaretz*, April 8, 2018.

23 Fredric Jameson, *The Political Unconscious: Narrative as a Socially Symbolic Act* (Cornell University Press, 1982).

24 Patrick Wolfe, "Settler Colonialism and the Elimination of the Native," *Journal of Genocide Research* 8, no. 4 (2006): 387–409.

25 Gideon Levy, "Israel, Where Is Your Outrage at the Legalisation of Apartheid?" *Middle East Eye*, July 26, 2018, middleeasteye.net.

26 Edward Said, "Zionism from the Standpoint of its Victims," in *The Question of Palestine* (Routledge / Kegan Paul, 1979), 56–83.

27 In his *The Biggest Prison on Earth: A History of the Occupied Territories,* Ilan Pappé argues, based on the IOF's archive that, "Israeli strategists discovered that if (they) want to continue their policy of ethnic cleansing after the Nakba, the alternative to expulsion is not to allow the people to leave the place where they live—and thus they can be excluded from the demographic balance of power. They are contained inside their own areas, but do not have to be counted in the overall national demographics since they cannot freely move, develop or expand, nor do they have any basic civil and human rights" (122).

28 Edward Said and Christopher Hitchens, *The History of Palestinian Exile and Diaspora* (Verso, 1988).

29 Edward Said, *Politics of Dispossession* (Vintage Books, 1995), 172.

30 Paulo Freire, *Pedagogy of the Oppressed* (Penguin Classics, 2017). The full text is available at historyisaweapon.com.

31 Philip Weiss, "America's Whiteness Crisis, and Zionism's," Opinion, *Mondoweiss*, January 10, 2021, mondoweiss.net.

32 Hagai El-Ad, "We Are Israel's Largest Human Rights Group—and

We Are Calling This Apartheid," *The Guardian*, January 12, 2021, theguardian.com.

33 "Israel Minister Calls for 'Ways More Painful than Death' for Palestinians," *Middle East Monitor,* January 6, 2024, middleeastmonitor.com.

34 Benny Morris, "Israel's Security Depends on Rafah," *New York Times*, April 11, 2024, nytimes.com.

35 Francesca Albanese, *The Question of Palestine: Anatomy of a Genocide. Report of the Special Rapporteur on the Situation of Human Rights in Palestinian Territories occupied since 1967*, United Nations, March 24, 2024, un.org.

36 Edward Said, *Orientalism* (Pantheon Books, 1978), 15.

37 "Ben Gvir Calls for Executing Palestinian Prisoners," *Middle East Monitor*, July 1, 2024, middleeastmonitor.com.

38 Amilcar Cabral, *Revolution in Guinea: Selected Texts* (Monthly Review Press, 2024).

INDEX

1948, xiv, 29, 54, 65, 141
1948 Genocide Convention, 104
2000, Intifada, 20
2006, elections, 73

Abbas, Mahmoud, 20, 62
Abu Akleh, Shireen, 188
Abu Alouf, Ayman, 127
Abu Arrar, Siba, 112
Abu el-Gheit, Ahmed, 25
Abu Jamei family, 37
Abu Malhous family, 116
Abu Ouf, Amara, xxii
Abu Saleh, Fadi, 90
Abu Sitta, Salman, 187
Abu Teir, Raed, 112
Abu Yahya, Khail, 184
Abu Zayd, Karen, 20
Abu Znaid, Maather, 37
academic institutions, 33–4. *See also* intellectuals; *individual universities*
Al Wehda Street massacre, xxv, 125–8
Al-Aqsa University, 66
Albanese, Francesca, 173
al-Haj, Najla, 38
al-Hussein, Zeid Raad, 94
All That is Left to You (Kanafani), 39, 182
al-Mashharawi, Omar, 25
al-Najjar, Razan, 93
al-Rimal neighbourhood, 143, 154–5
al-Shifa hospital, 144, 172
al-Udini, Ahmed, 90
ambulances, 42
American Studies Association (ASA), 33, 34
"America's Whiteness Crisis, and Zionism's" (Weiss), 157, 159
annexation, 119, 120
antisemitism, 86, 134–5
apartheid: and B'Tselem, 158; defined, 18; and genocide, 19, 140; and Israel's birth, xiii–xiv; normalizing, 69, 148; Palestine overview, 18–19; and Palestinian intellectuals, 13; as racism, 18, 19–20, in South Africa, 10–11, 51, 117–18, 158–9 (*see also* South Africa); strength of resistance, 59–60
Arab League, xxi, 80
Arab regimes: 2009 siege reaction, 5; 2018 siege reaction, 91; 2024 genocide reaction, 178–9, 191; as giving up on Palestine, 147; and October 7, 2023 retaliation, 150–1; Palestine position

overview, 5–6; and West, 163. *See also* Egypt
Arab Spring, 25–6
Arafat, Ranan, 25
Arafat, Yasser, 120, 188
Arendt, Hannah, 161, 162
assimilation, 10
Austin, Lloyd, 145

Bantustans, 10, 17, 18, 19, 20, 38, 43, 60, 67, 69, 99, 109, 119, 153, 190; West Bank as, 98
Barak, Ehud, 190
Baraka, Ajamu, 135
Begin, Menachem, 83
Ben-Givr, Itamar, 135, 182
Benjamin, Walter, 42
Biden, Joe: election 2021, 157; and humanity of Palestinians, 129; and ICC, 158; Palestine vs. S. Africa, 126; supporting war crimes, 141; and Trump, 159; as Zionist, 160
The Biggest Prison on Earth (Pappé), 140, 196n27
Biko, Steve, 51, 60
"Birds Die in Galilee" (Darwish), 28
blame, 10, 44, 67, 82–3
Blinken, Antony, 145, 190
blockade: 2018, 104; 2024, 173; and ceasefires, 113; construction materials, 65; and genocide, 68; lifting, 136; rationale behind, 75; since election of 2006, 20, 61–3
Bolivia, 49
borders in 1967, 55
boycott, divestment, and sanctions in S. Africa, 6
Boycott, Divestment, Sanctions (BDS): overview, xxi–xxii, 34–5, 48, 77; and academic institutions, 33–4; and Arab countries, 25; and Great March of Return, 101; importance of, 68, 78; as isolation, 51; Israel's reaction to, 58–60; as victorious, 60; as window of hope, 95
Britain, 47
B'Tselem, 158

Cabral, Amilcar, 149, 183
Camp David Accords, 25, 54, 120, 148, 190
Carter, Jimmy, 83, 133
ceasefires: 2019, 112–13; 2024, 179, 190–1; and blockades, 113; and ICJ compliance, 168
children: 1987, 37; 2006–2014, 59; 2009, 3–4, 38; 2012, 25; 2018, 93; 2019, 112; 2023, 141, 150; 2024, 172; as targets, 41, 42, 46, 129
citizenship, 87–8, 97–8
civic assassination, 58, 59
class consciousness, 11. *See also* intellectuals
Clinton, Hillary, 15
colonialism: overview, 125–6; Eastern European settlers, 187; and genocide, 19, 174; history of, 56; vs. liberation, 141; normalizing, 69; Said on, 190. *See also* decolonization
constitution, 88
construction materials, 65
contamination, 105. *See also* water
co-option, 11
corporations, 42

Dahiya doctrine, 128–9
Dahlan, Muhammad, 68
Darwish, Mahmoud, 28

Day of Rage, 49, 52
decolonization, 11, 140
defeatist perspective, 10–12, 50
dehydration, 144
Deir Yassin massacre, 116
demands from Palestinians, 111, 145
democracy, 34, 54
Democratic Fronts for the Liberation of Palestine (DFLP), 100
Deri, Aryeh, 58
dis-participation, 68
displaced people, 150, 172. *See also* refugees
doctors/paramedics, 114, 128. *See also* hospitals; medical care
drones, 37

education, 33–4, 75
Egypt, 25, 68, 113, 147, 149. *See also* Arab regimes
Eid, Amneh Abdullah Ahmed, 28–30
Eid, Ashraf, 37
Eid, Hafez Abdulhafez, 30
Eid, Haidar: about, xiv, xxv; friends and family killed, 37–8, 155–6, 181, 184; in Gaza 2000, 74; as honest partisan, xviii–xix; inspiration of, xix; leaving Gaza, 154–6; life in Palestine, 59; refuge in South Africa, xxi, 154, 156; as refugee, xvii, xxv, 175; survivors guilt, 185; university degree, 73; vision of, xvi–xvii, xxi–xxii, 141–2
Eisenkot, Gadi, 129
El Areer, Refaat, 184
El Bursh, Adnan, 184
El Farra, Reem, 184
El-Ad, Hagai, 158
elections 2006, 73
electricity, 59, 61, 91, 143
El-Ghandour, Laila, 90
Eliyahu, Amichai, 166
Eluard, Paul, 36
equality, 141
Erdan, Gilad, 94
Eretz checkpoint, 74
"Eretz Israel" ideology, 56
ESCWA report, 80
ethnic cleansing, 140. *See also* genocide
Euro-Med Human Rights Monitor, 172
Europe, 146, 187. *See also* international community; Western nations
Eurovision song contest, 113, 114
evacuation, 144

Fairouz, 78
Falasteen, 175
Falk, Richard, xiii–xxiii, 63, 82
Fanon, Frantz, 9
Fatah, 66–7, 101. *See also* Palestinian Authority
The Fate of the Jews (Feuerlicht), xxv
Feuerlicht, Roberta Strauss, xxv
fire belt, 154
First Intifada, 74, 100
Firwana, Omar, 143
fishing, 75
food insecurity, 75, 144
Foucault, Michel, 9
Fourth Geneva Convention, 111, 135
Freire, Paulo, 142

Gallant, Yoav, 146

Gandhi, Mahatma, 60
Gantz, Benny, 117, 133, 136
Gaza: in 2000, 73–4; in 2005, 74, 132; in 2006, 132; in 2008, 161; overview, 83; borders in 1967, 55; as concentration camp, xiv, 20, 69–70, 132–3; death as daily routine, 63; as decaying, 105; de-development, 75; electricity in, 59, 61–3, 91, 143; GDP, 62–3; as isolated, 19; mainstream media portrayal of, xxvi; as prison, 16; Safe Passage, 74; size of, 36, 73; starvation, 63 (*see also* food insecurity); unemployment in, 62–3, 75; walls in, 74, 98, 132–3; water in, 59, 61–3, 91, 143.
See also Israel; Palestine; Palestinians; *specific dates and topics*
GDP, 62–3.
genocide: and 1948 Genocide Convention, 104; and apartheid, 19, 140; and colonialism, 174; vs. exploitation, 20; as incremental, 61, 63, 76; and intent, xv; and Lieberman, 17; as Netanyahu's distraction, 189; normalizing, 162, 163; objectives of, 186–7; protests against, 163; and religion/ethnicity, 80; and right of return, 43; as word, xiv–xv. *See also* International Court of Justice
Genocide Convention (1948), 104
Ghebreyesus, Tedros Adhanom, 172
Goldstone, Richard, 104
Goldstone Report, 16, 104
Gramsci, Antonio, xx
Great March of Return, 89–92, 94, 100–3, 108–9, 114, 126
Gurion, Ben, 45
Guterres, Antonio, 185

Habibi, Emile, 184–5
Hague Convention, 135
Hallaque, Akram, 42–3
Hamas: and blockade, 61–2; and Dahlan, 68; and development, 63; elections 2006, 12; and Great March of Return, 101; Israel on, 4–5; Israel-Hamas dichotomy, 10; and occupation history, 185; and Palestinian Authority victory, 20, 66; Palestinian leaders on, 8, 10; Palestinian people as, 82–3; and protests, 82–3, 94; as "terrorists," xv
Hirbya (Zikim), 141
Holocaust, 50, 53, 134–5, 161–2
homes/buildings destroyed, 21, 56, 83, 105–6, 172
hospitals, 15, 91, 144
Huj (Sderot), 141
humanitarian aid, 20
hunger strikes, 55

inclusivity, 51
incremental genocide, 61, 63, 76. *See also* genocide
independence vs. liberation, 142
innocence, 76
intellectuals, 9–12, 13, 33, 75
International Committee of the Red Cross (ICRC), 62
international community: overview, xvi; and collaboration, 69; as deaf, 135; demands for Palestinians, 111; as failing, 63–4; Gaza in 2008, 162; and

ICJ ruling, 170–1; and liberation vision, 141; and Nazi regime, 162; and neutrality, 96; Pilger's views, 143; and S. Africa, 76–7; support as expected, 142; support as important, 78–9
International Court of Justice (ICJ), xxiii, 164, 167–71. *See also* Boycott, Divestment, Sanctions; Europe; silence; United States; Western nations
International Criminal Court (ICC), 158
International Humanitarian Law, 111
Intifada (2000), 20
Intifada stone, 189–90
Islamophobia, xx
Israel: in 1948, 29; overview, 45, 56; and Abbas, 62; as admired by racists, 157, 159; ambulances and casualties, 37, 42; army details, 54, 90; and Bantustans, 19; Basic Laws, 157–8; and Biden (*see* Biden, Joe); bombing/aggression (*see* Gaza); and borders in 1967, 55; children as targets, 41, 42, 46, 129; citizenship, 87–8, 97–8; as collapsing, 189; constitution, 88; controlled massacre, 79; critiques by S. Africa, 83 (*see also* ICJ complaint); Dahiya doctrine, 128–9; defending itself, 129; disengagement 2005, xiv; and Egypt, 25; endgame of, 116; "Eretz Israel" ideology, 56; and ICJ complaint, xxiii, 164, 167–71; intellectuals, 33; and international community (*see* international community); and international law, 56; and January 6 attacks, 157; Jewish citizens as Zionist, 140; as Jewish state, 12, 96; and Judaism, 54; in Lebanon, 8; and mainstream media, 45–6; and Obama (*see* Obama, Barak); objectives of war, 151–2, 186–7; Orientalism of, 134; and Oslo Accords, 56; and Palestine election 2006, 73; and Palestine resistance, 47; and Palestinian state, 12, 43; position in 2014, 43; power imbalance, 112–13, 129; and Rafah, 173; as settler colony (*see* colonialism); shoot to kill policy, 74; soldiers killed 2024, 174; transformation of, 34; and UN Human Rights Council probe, 94; and UN Security Council, 76; and the West (*see* Western nations); "withdrawal" in 2005, 74; withdrawal from Strip, 106. *See also* Boycott, Divestment, Sanctions; Gaza; Palestine; Palestinians; Zionism; *individual politicians*
Israel-Hamas dichotomy, 10

Jameson, Fredric, 87
January 6 attacks (US), 157
Jerusalem, 89
Jewish supremacy, 158. *See also* Zionism
Jim Crow, 158–9
journalists, 114. *See also* mainstream media
justice, 141

Kanafani, Ghassan, xxvi–xxvii, 39, 181–2
Kasrils, Ronnie, 50, 83

Kathrada, Ahmed, 83
Katz, Israel, 58–9
Kedar, Mordechai, 41
Khalidi, Rashid, xviii
King, Martin Luther King, 125
Knesset, Israeli, 96
Kochavi, Avi, 175

laws, xiv, xix, 56
Lebanon, 8, 191
Lemkin Institute for Genocide Prevention, 173
Levy, Gideon, 61, 63, 80, 107
liberation: vs. coordination, 39; vs. independence, 9, 12, 142, 148–9
liberation vision, xvi–xvii, xxi–xxii, 141–2
"Liberty" (Eluard), 36
Lieberman, Avigdor, 17, 25, 82–3
Livni, Tzipi, 4
Lukács, György, 11

mainstream media: control of, 42; explanations to, 125; Gazans' portrayal in, xxvi; and Israel, 45–6, 54; as "objective," 53, 56–7; and political prisoners, 55; silence of (*see* silence); the West and context, xiv; White House photo op 1993, xviii
Makdisi, Saree, 20
Make America Great Again (MAGA), 158–60
Mandela, Nelson, 60, 95, 125
March of Return. *See* Great March of Return
martyrs, 36, 90, 181
Marxist–Leninists, 100
mass graves, 172
Mdoukh, Saadi, 181
media. *See* mainstream media
medical care, 83, 105, 114, 143, 169, 181. *See also* hospitals
Meir, Golda, 45
Men in the Sun (Kanafani), xxvi–xxvii, 39, 182, 192
miscarriages, 169
mobilization, xxii
Morales, Evo, 49
morality, 4
Morris, Benny, 173
"mow the lawn," xvii, 46, 50–1
Muhammad, Rashid, 3–4, 37
Muhammad, Samir, 37

Najd, 14–15
Nakba: Eid personal reflections, 28–30; and Guterres, 185; and later generations, 70; as ongoing, 56; seventieth anniversary, 84
Naksa, 139–40. *See also* Israel
Nasser, Gamal Abdel, 147, 149
Nasser Hospital, 172
national project, 66–7
nationality, 87–8
nation-state law, 96
Nazis, 162. *See also* Holocaust
Netanyahu, Benjamin: and Ben-Gvir and Smotrich, 135; and civilians, 112; fraud of, 189; and Gantz, 117; and Obama, 15; power and genocide, 189; UNGA map, xv
neutrality, 96
non-governmental organizations (NGOs), 9. *See also* intellectuals
nonviolent measures, 78. *See also* Boycott, Divestment, Sanctions
nuclear bombs, 166
Nuseirat Refugee Camp, xvii, 30, 175–6

Obama, Barak, 14–17, 55
occupation defined, 54, 140
October 7, 2023, xiv
October 7, 2023 retaliation: as of October 15, 2023, 143–4; as of Nov. 2023, 150; as of May 1, 2024, 172; as of June 9, 2024, 176; as of June 28, 2024, 178; as of July 13, 2024, 182; one year anniversary, 184–8; as of December 3, 2023, 154–6; and Eid leaving Palestine, 154–6; as of May 1, 2024, 172; as of October 30, 2023, 150; and Palestinian demands, 145; and silence of Arab regimes, 149
Olmert, Ehud, 4–5
One Democratic State Campaign, 120
one state solution, xvi–xvii, xxi–xxii, 102. *See also* liberation vision
open-air prison: Gaza as, xxv, 16, 63, 65, 70, 73, 74, 94, 106, 117, 176
oranges, 176
Organisation of Islamic Cooperation, 80
Orientalism, 134
Orientalism (Said), 174
Oslo Process/Accords: about, 8–9†; and balance of power, 56; and confinement, 73–4; and Eid, xvi–xvii; and Fatah, 67–8; February 2009, 8–9; and Gaza in 2014, 42; and Great March of Return, 102; and Palestinian state, 12; and Palestinian intellectuals, 9; and Palestinian leaders, 103; and Palestinian rejection, 55; and right of return, 9†, 55; as slavery, 39–40; as war machine, 187–8
Palestine: in 1948, xiv, 29, 54, 65, 141; as alone, 178; and Camp David Accords, 25†; and Clinton, 15; demilitarizing, xix–xx; dependence on Israeli products, 56; and Egypt, 25, 27; elections 2006, 12; history of, 139–41; homes/buildings destroyed, 21, 172; and Netanyahu's UNGA map, xv; and optimism, xx; and S. Africa freedom, 60; and S. Africa similarities, 18–19, 27, 50–2, 91, 98–9 (*see also* apartheid; Gaza)
Palestinian Authority (PA), 20, 54, 62, 66–7
Palestinian Democratic Union, 100
Palestinian leaders: overview, xviii, xix; and autonomy of people, 60; measures to follow, 152; and Oslo Accords, 103; and power of the people, 101
Palestinian Liberation Organization (PLO), xviii, 8–9, 67, 120
Palestinian National Initiative, 100
Palestinian People's Party, 100
Palestinians: collective memory of, 46–7; deaths 2009, 3–7; deaths 2014, 48, 59; deaths 2018, 79, 82, 93; deaths 2023, 141, 144, 150, 163, 165; deaths 2024, 168, 172, 176, 182; deaths and news, 63; demands for Palestinians, 111, 145; as fighting, 91; as foreigners, 97–8; as Hamas, 82–3; history of, 53; and humanitarian aid, 20; as infiltrators, 93–4; intellectuals, 9–12, 13; power imbalance,

112–13, 129; in prison, 55; right of return (*see* right of return); terminally ill people, 15–16; and Universal Declaration of Human Rights, 85; wounds of, 83; and Zionism, 86–7. *See also* Gaza
Pappé, Ilan, 63, 140, 169–70, 196n27
peace process, xiv, xviii, 86
people vs. leaders, xxi–xxii, 6
Pessoptomism, 184–5
Pilger, John, 143
political prisoners, 55
Politics of Dispossession (Said), 134
Popular Front for the Liberation of Palestine (PLO), 100
popular resistance, 101
poverty, 75
prison, 34. *See also* open-air prison
prisoners, 182
protests: 2014, 49, 52; 2018, 82, 84, 89–92; on campuses, xix; deaths at, 90, 108; against genocide, 163; and Hamas, 82–3, 94; Intifada stone, 189–90; and Israel army, 90, 93; and racism, 94. *See also* Boycott, Divestment, Sanctions; Great March of Return

Qirm, Amira, 4, 38
Qirm, Ismat, 38

racism: and apartheid, 18, 19–20; of Begin and Shamir, 83; and inhumane actions, 50; Orientalism of Israel, 134; and protests, 94; of West, 146; as worldview of Israel, 94–5; of Zionism, 96–7, 157–8. *See also* Islamophobia
Rafah, 173
Rafah crossing, 105, 136
rape, 41
Rashid, Haroon Hashem, 78
Reagan, Ronald, 95
Refugees: Eid as, xvii, xxi, xxv, 154, 156, 175 (*see also* right of return); *Men in the Sun*, xxvi–xxvii; numbers in 2009, 16; numbers in 2017, 65; numbers in 2018, 88; numbers in 2024, 187; numbers in 2105, 49; ratio of, 141
resistance movements (general): critics on, 10; decolonization of, 11, 140; and occupation, 54
Resolution 194 (1948), xiv, xvi, 16, 43, 55, 83, 89, 94, 100, 103, 117, 141, 185,
responsibility, 141, 143. *See also* blame
Returning to Haifa (Kanafani), 182
right of return: and Camp David Accords, 25† (*see also* refugees); and Eid, xvii; and genocide, 43; Great March of Return, 89–92, 94, 100–3, 114; and Israel, 43; number of refugees, 141; and Oslo Accords, 9†, 55, 109; Palestinians vs. Jews, xiv; and peace, 86; Resolution 194 (1948), xiv, 141; vs. two-state solution, 109, 185
Roy, Sara, 105

Sadat, Anwar, 147
Safe Passage, 74
Said, Edward: on 1948, 29; on blaming the victim, 134–5; on colonialism, 190; on democratic

Left, 11; on European culture, 174; on morality, 26; and Obama, 14, 16; Palestinian narrative, 36, 188
Samouni, Muhammad, 4, 38
Samouni, Subhi, 3
schools, 82
Sderot (Huj), 14–15, 141
self-government, 109. *See also* two-state solution
settlements, 15
settler colonialism. *See* colonialism
Shamir, Yitzhak, 83, 119
Sharon, Ariel, 191
Sharpeville Massacre (South Africa), 6
Shin Bet, 74
shoah. *See* Holocaust
shoah, as word, 161–2
Shujayea, 48–9
silence: of Arab League, xxi; on Gaza 2009, 6; on Gaza 2018, 91; on Gaza 2023, 144–5, 149, 165–7; on Gaza 2024, 179; of mainstream media, 63; Pilger on, 143
Smotrich, Bezalel, 135
Soffer, Arnon, 49–50, 166
South Africa: Bantustans, 10, 17, 18, 19, 38, 119; boycott, divestment, and sanctions, 6, 95; critiques of Israel, 83; Eid family refuge in, xxi, 154; and First Intifada, 100; four pillars of struggle, 10–11; ICJ complaint, xxiii, 164, 167–71; and international community, 76–7; and Palestine freedom, 60; and Palestine similarities, 18–19, 27, 50–2, 91, 98–9 (*see also* apartheid); as uncompromising, 119
Spain, 49
Stalinist Left, 100
starvation, 15–16, 63. *See also* food insecurity
Steinitz, Yuval, 94–5
“Stop BDS” Conference, 58
support, 48, 51–2, 78–8, 78–9, 142. *See also* Boycott, Divestment, Sanctions
surveillance, 132–3

terminally ill people, 15–16
“terrorism,” xv
Thabet, Tasneem, 184
Thatcher, Margaret, 95
Trump, Donald, xix, 157–60
Tutu, Desmond, 6, 20, 83
“two sides,” xxii
two-state solution: overview, xix–xx; barriers to, 16–17; and Great March of Return, 102–3; independence vs. liberation, 12; killed in 2020, 119; vs. right of return, 109, 185

Ukraine, 142
UN Fact-Finding Mission (2009), 104
UN General Assembly (UNGA), xv
UN Human Rights Council probe, 94
UN resolutions, 55
UN Security Council, 76
unemployment, 62–3, 75
United Arab Emirates, 68
United Nations, 62, 75, 113. *See also* Resolution 194
United Nations Relief and Works Agency (UNRWA), 82, 105, 173
United States: and corporations,

42; and Egypt, 147; embassy, 89; and Great March of Return, 126; January 6 attacks, 157; legitimate vs. terrorist attacks, 190; missiles made in, 39; and Oslo Process, xviii; and Palestine election 2006, 73; power of, 147; racism of, 158–9; and radicalism in Middle East, 191; weaponry, 178. *See also* Biden, Joe; international community; Obama, Barak; Western nations
unity, 101–2
Universal Declaration of Human Rights, 85
University of Johannesburg, 73–4

Vilnai, Matan, 83, 161

walls/fences, 74, 98, 132–3
war crimes, 102–3, 113, 141, 145, 146
water, 59, 61, 91, 143
Wehda Street massacre, xxv, 125–8
Weiss, Philip, 157, 159
Weissglass, Dov, 75
West Bank, 119, 129, 189
Western nations: overview, 145–6; and "genocide" as word, xiv–xv; as hegemonic, 174; media and context, xiv; as neutral, 151; and Palestinian agency, 11; and "two sides," xxii; and war crimes, 145, 146; as warring, 162–3. *See also* Europe; international community; mainstream media; United States
whataboutism, 135
white supremacy, 157, 158–9, 177
whitewashing, 113, 114
Wolfe, Patrick, 106
The Work of Art in the Age of Mechanical Reproduction (Benjamin), 42

Yaalon, Moshe, 50, 129

Zarnouqa, 29–30, 37, 175–6
Zikim (Hirbya), 141
Zionism. *See also* Israel: overview, 86–7, 96–7; antithesis of, 51; and civil liberties, 97; end of, 97; extending, 108; of Jewish citizens, 140; and killing, 50; vs. liberation, 141; and Palestinians, 86–7; as racist, 96–7; and "two sides," xxii

HAIDAR EID is an associate professor of postcolonial and postmodern literature at Al-Aqsa University in Gaza, Palestine and a research associate at the Centre for Asian Studies at the University of Pretoria, South Africa. He is a policy advisor with *Al-Shabaka*, the Palestinian Policy Network, on the advisory board of the Palestinian Campaign for the Academic and Cultural Boycott of Israel (PACBI), and a member of the Board of Directors of BADIL Resource Center for Palestinian Residency and Refugee Rights. He is the author of *Worlding Postmodernism: Interpretive Possibilities of Critical Theory*, *Countering the Palestinian Nakba: One State for All*, and *Decolonizing the Palestinian Mind.*